Anxiety of Words

Anxiety of Words

Contemporary Poetry by Korean Women

최승자	Ch'oe Sŭng-ja
김혜순	Kim Hyesoon
이연주	Yi Yŏn-ju

TRANSLATED BY *Don Mee Choi*

ZEPHYR PRESS
Brookline, MA

Cover painting "Yi Pok-nam" by Ahn Il Soon. Originally shown in 2002,
        in the Hankuk Art Museum.
Interior painting by Yi Yŏn-ju
Excerpt from "Tenebrae" by Paul Celan, from *Poems of Paul Celan*,
        translated by Michael Hamburger, reprinted by permission
        of Persea Books.
Book design by *typeslowly*
Printed in Michigan by Cushing-Malloy, Inc.

Zephyr Press, a non-profit arts and education 501(c)(3) organization, publishes
literary titles that foster deeper understanding of cultures and languages.
Zephyr books are distributed to the trade in the U.S. and Canada by Con-
sortium Book Sales and Distribution [www.cbsd.com] and by Small Press
Distribution [www.spdbooks.org].

Library of Congress Cataloging-in-Publication Data

Ch'oe, Sung-ja.
  [Poems. English & Korean. Selections]
  Anxiety of words : contemporary poetry by Korean women / Ch'oe Sŭng-ja,
Kim Hyesoon, and Yi Yŏn-ju ; translated by Don Mee choi. -- 1st ed.
      p. cm.
  In English and Korean.
  Includes bibliographical references.
  ISBN 0-939010-87-9 (alk. paper)
  1. Ch'oe, Sŭng-ja--Translations into English. 2. Kim, Hye-sun--Translations
into English. 3. Yi, Yŏn-ju, 1953-1992--Translations into English. 4. Women
poets, Korean--Translations into English. 5. Korean poetry--20th century-
-Translations into English. I. Kim, Hye-sun. Poems. English & Korean.
Selections II. Yi, Yŏn-ju, 1953-1992. Poems. English & Korean. Selections III.
Choi, Don Mee. IV. Title.
  PL992.18.S7A2 2006
  895.7'15--dc22

                              2006024686

98765432 first edition in 2006

ZEPHYR PRESS
50 Kenwood Street
Brookline, MA 02446
www.zephyrpress.org

Acknowledgments

The translation of this project was supported by a generous grant from the Korea Literature Translation Institute, Seoul. This book has been published with the assistance of the Korea Literature Translation Institute, the Massachusetts Cultural Council and the National Endowment for the Arts.

massculturalcouncil.org

NATIONAL
ENDOWMENT
FOR THE ARTS

Grateful acknowledgment is made to the editors of the following publications, in which some of these translations originally appeared:

Arirang: "An Automatic Film Processor," "Taklamakan," "The Phone Rings Endlessly," "For Suk," "The Dictator," "Prostitute 4"

Artful Dodge: "A Family Photo," "Festival of Waste," "A Report on the Unconsciousness of the Masses"

Arts & Letters: "Words 1 & 2," "A Song," "Regarding Love"

Bamboo Ridge: "Our Love of 197x," "Don't Want to Eat Today's Dinner"

Cipher Journal: "A Room with Drawn Blinds," Inside My Eyes," "A Riverside Food Stall"

The G.W. Review: "Went to the Sea in Winter," "Untitled 2"

Gargoyle: "Prostitute 7," "An Executioner Doesn't Have the Time to Read a Letter"

Korean Literature Today: "Confession," "Practice," Regarding Women," "Regarding Love 2," "To Patients with Contagious Diseases," "Song of Skin"

The Literary Review: "A Question Mark"

The Massachusetts Review: "Father is Too Heavy, What Do I do?"

Prairie Schooner: "To Become Tiny as a Cricket," "You," "Memories of Giving Birth to a Daughter"

Seneca Review: "From a Place Where I Can't Call You as You," "Untitled 1," "For Y"

The Spoon River Poetry Review: "La La La, There is No Way of Knowing," "A Tiresome Dialog," "For Kanamycin"

Tinfish: "Rain," "The Princess of Seoul Has Just Awoken," "A Very Old Hotel"

Table of Contents

Ch'oe Sŭng-ja

Kim Hyesoon

Yi Yŏn-ju

An Anxiety of Words

My formal study of twentieth-century Korean literature began in 1998, soon after meeting Bruce and Ju-chan Fulton in Seattle at a reading of their book of translations, *Wayfarer: New Fiction by Korean Women.* Shortly thereafter, I was introduced to two papers that would lead me to the study of poetry. Bruce Fulton's unpublished paper, "Images of Women in Modern Korean Women's Poetry," addressed how, since the 1920s, Korean women poets have defied traditional Korean gender roles by participating in a literary tradition publicly permitted only to men in the pre-modern era. When I was given a copy of an essay, "The Achievements and Prospects of Modern Korean Women's Poetry," by Kim Chŏng-nan, delivered at the University of California, Los Angeles, in 1996, I learned of the emergence of a feminist consciousness in women's poetry beginning in the 1970s.

These two papers raised my curiosity about contemporary Korean women's poetry, and how Korean feminist poets differed from the women I had known in Korea. While I was growing up in South Korea, the only women that I was close to were my mother, grandmothers, and aunts. They farmed, raised children, and struggled to give their children a better life, having been uprooted and devastated by the Korean War. My grandmothers and aunts told me old Korean folk stories. What stories do the Korean women poets tell? In 1972, while still a child, I left South Korea for Hong Kong with my immediate family, and did not fully understand that my family had left South Korea to escape political oppression. When I read Kim Chŏng-nan's paper, I couldn't help but ask, how did people survive the oppression? And how did Korean women gain a feminist consciousness under military dictatorships?

My answer, in part, came through the poetry of three poets, Ch'oe Sŭng-ja (b. 1952), Kim Hyesoon (b. 1955), and Yi Yŏn-ju (1953-1992). Their poetry emerged in the 1980s during one of the most politically harsh periods of contemporary Korean history. At first I was unable to articulate my initial attraction to their poetry. I simply knew that I connected intuitively to their words and felt an urge to translate them into English. Later, I came to understand that what attracted me were their fierce and innovative poetic voices, and their critical consciousness of Korean women's lives under patriarchy, capitalism, and neocolonialism. As I began translating their work, I was able to reconnect with my original home. The translation process enabled me to create a bridge through which I could return home and understand the two locations—my place of origin and my new home in the U.S. I came to understand that my dislocation was born out of these two locations of unequal power.

* * *

Prior to U.S. intervention and getting caught in the global "class war" between capitalist and socialist nation-states after World War II—which led to the division of Korea into North and South—Korea was under Japanese colonial rule from 1910 to 1945. The Korean War of 1950-1953 was devastating—over 2 million civilians and combatants were killed. Next, South Korea endured a string of military dictatorships in the 1960s-80s. Only since 1993 has South Korea had a civilian government. The brutal dictatorships of President Park Chung Hee (1961-79) and President Chun Doo Hwan (1980-87), supported by the U.S., suppressed many dissenting workers, students, and intellectuals, and included the military massacre of students and civilians during the pro-democratic rebellions of 1960 and 1980. Such internal oppression is what the Nigerian writer Ken Saro-Wiwa calls "monstrous domestic colonialism," which is an aspect of neocolonialism. The neocolonial relations between South Korea and the U.S. entailed massive amounts of cash and military aid between 1945-65, and the presence of an estimated 35,000 U.S. troops and 100 military bases and installations that are still in operation. Another aspect of neocolonialism in South Korea was the exploitation of women, particularly poor, rural women. Korea was one of the main suppliers of cheap labor for Japan and the U.S. during Korea's industrialization under Park's two decades of military rule. Export-led industries such as electronics, textiles and clothing, and other light industries, employed mostly women. By the 1970s, young women carried out most of the labor-intensive light industrial work, toiling an average of 15 hours a day in sweatshops. The deplorable situations in the sweatshops still exist today; Korean women workers simply have been replaced by migrant workers from South and Southeast Asian countries, including Koreans who had settled permanently in China prior to the Korean War, while Korea was under Japanese control.

* * *

In the 1970s and 80s "national literature" (*minjok munhak*) and "people's literature" (*minjung munhak*) dominated South Korea's literary scene. National literature was a part of a self-determination and decolonizing movement that addressed the need to overcome Korea's national division and social contradictions. People's literature—an outgrowth of national literature—was concerned with those most oppressed by Korea's authoritarian government and the process of industrialization. These movements were dominated by men, and the literary resistance was part of a larger political, social, and cultural populist movement called the "people or the masses" (*minjung*) movement.

South Korean women's resistance was an important aspect of the *minjung* movement. Like the Korean women's socialist feminism of the 1930s, the feminism of the 1970s and 80s connected issues of class, gender, and nation as a challenge to women's oppression. Its beginnings can be traced to women's labor struggles of the 1970s such as the independent union activity led by the mother of Chŏn T'ae-il, a worker who self-immolated himself in 1970 to protest the horrific conditions of garment factory workers.

Kim Hyesoon is an active member of the feminist organization, Another Culture (*Ttohana ŭi munhwa*), and she advanced Korean women's literature through her poetry and criticism, which has appeared in Another Culture's publications. Yi Yŏn-ju was not a member of any political or women's organization, but, according to an interview I conducted with her brother, she was a nurse who worked and served in the most economically impoverished communities in South Korea. She worked in mining and farming towns, including Ŭijŏngbu, located near a U.S. military base, where many women and children are trapped in devastating conditions of poverty, military prostitution, and social alienation. Now, most of the women involved in prostitution near the bases are trafficked in from Russia and the

Philippines. It is evident through Yi's life that she had a strong *minjung* consciousness and was committed to service. And Ch'oe Sŭng-ja was the first woman student editor of her university's literary journal, through which she promoted women's voices. She was also the first woman to publish her poetry in one of South Korea's leading journals of dissent in the 1970s and 80s, *Literature and Intellect* (*Munhak kwa chisŏng*). Many of her abrasive poems were aimed at South Korea's corrupt dictatorships and capitalism, and the government's willing subordinate stance to the U.S. Ch'oe's literary life and poetry challenged many boundaries that have kept women silent on literary, social, and political levels.

Ko Chŏng-hŭi (1948-1991), a contemporary poet who precedes Ch'oe, Kim, and Yi, was also a member of Another Culture and played a leading role in publishing feminist literature and criticism. Another Culture's publication dedicated its third issue to "Feminist Literature" in 1995. But discussions on the topic had begun earlier, in 1986, with Ko's groundbreaking essay, "The Development of Korean Women's Literature," and with the gathering of prominent poets and writers such as Ko and Pak Wan-sŏ and other feminist activists and scholars in 1987. At the 1987 gathering, the concept of feminist literature was widely explored and defined in the context of a women's resistance that gave voice to women's social and historical conditions, and, therefore, it was understood as a "literature of indictment," and a part of *minjung* literature.

In 2001, I interviewed Kim Hyesoon and Ch'oe Sŭng-ja about their poetry, including its relationship to current and past political and literary trends. Kim Hyesoon said that in the context of *minjung* literature, her poetry did not resist directly: "What I wrote about was cooking and my ingredient was death ... I tried to turn the heaviness of oppression into something playful and light, so that what I ended up with was a type of poetry that did not appear to be political." She also has written that throughout the 1980s Korean literary critics demanded that she "enter the sea of society" and write poetry that can "communicate and benefit society." But at the same time, they stated that a "woman poet is nature" who must "evoke something gentle and motherly." Kim believes that such contradictory demands marginalized women poets over the past few decades: "The father of women poets at this time was a single father who enforced a triple form of oppression on women: a father who oppressed an individual socially and politically, who crushed gender equality, and who mandated that women form their identity from the margins."

Two women poets who preceded Ch'oe, Kim, and Yi deserve mentioning—Mun Chŏng-hŭi (b. 1947) and Kang Ŭn-gyo (b. 1946). In her essay, "The Achievements and Prospects of Modern Korean Women's Poetry," Kim Chŏng-nan notes that these two poets emerged in the 1970s with a critical feminist awareness and brought about a radical shift in women's poetry. Mun and Kang both dealt with images of women's bodies, flesh (*sal*), in their poetry—not in abstract or conceptual terms, but in concrete, existential ways that had previously been taboo in women's poetry. Kim Chŏng-nan states that the images of flesh in these poets must also be interpreted in the political context of the 1970s; images of the flesh are encoded with women's opposition to President Park's military rule.

It became clear to me, when talking with Ch'oe Sŭng-ja in 2001, that the political events that unfolded in the 1970s and 80s had a tremendous effect on her poetry. Ch'oe remembers being awakened early in the morning by a phone call from her close friend right after word had gotten out of Park Chung Hee's assassination. She remembers the exhilarating sense of liberation she felt when she heard "Park is dead!" However, this sense of liberation, felt nation-wide, immediately dissipated under the far more repressive rule of Chun Doo Hwan. She said that she did not consciously set out to be a feminist poet but that all the oppression that had been building in her simply exploded whenever she wrote. This explosion is evident in her poetry, through her "rough" language that is so unconventional for women poets, and her references to decay and the death of women's bodies.

The Korean poet that Kim Hyesoon most admires is Ch'oe. They quickly became friends as they were the only women poets present in the literary circles and debates of the 1980s. Kim was working as a literary editor and remembers how a book of plays she intended to publish came back censored from the military government. Everything was blackened out with ink except for the title and the name of the author. As in Ch'oe's work and in that of her predecessors, Mun and Kang, the experiences and expressions of the body are prominent in Kim's work. In my interview with Kim, she distinguished how Korean women's poetry differs from men's: "One of the characteristics of Korean men's poetry is that the poets don't handle their subject matters with their bodies. They handle their subjects only with their eyes. Whenever they see a landscape they freely carve out what they want from it. After they cut out a part, they describe it and then add aphorisms. There is a long tradition of this form of contemporary Korean men's poetry. Women, in general, let nature and their own natures be, so that both entities continue to exist on their own. And from this perspective they speak about the meetings and interactions between both through the object of their bodies. Women poets oppose and resist their conditions, using unconventional forms of language because their resistance has led them to a language that is unreal, surreal, and even fantastical. The language of women's poetry is internal, yet defiant and revolutionary."

Yi Yŏn-ju depicts the dehumanization of the body and the oppressed and exploited lives of women who are on the outer fringes of Korean society: women in poverty, women as cheap and exploited laborers, women exploited by government-sponsored sex tourism to attract Japanese men in the 1970s, and women trapped in the military prostitution of American military camp towns. Yi's poetry displays a penetrating awareness of Korean women's reality that intersects between gender, class, and nation. Unfortunately, outside her poetry, Yi was unable to defy the despair; she committed suicide in 1992, a year after publishing her first book of poems. According to her brother, she had contemplated suicide for many years and attempted it several times. Yi's anguish was not only personal but societal. She doubted the worthiness of life under such conditions.

Kim Hyesoon, Ch'oe Sŭng-ja, and Yi Yŏn-ju belong to the *hangŭl* generation. They were born in the 1950s, after the Japanese occupation, and thus they were educated only in vernacular Korean, *hangŭl*, a writing system which was promulgated in 1446 for women and commoners. Bruce Fulton points out that this is highly significant: *hangŭl* was the written and oral literary language of a majority of pre-modern Korean women. Its use allows for the historical transmission of a pre-modern feminist consciousness that reasserts itself in the written and oral literature of contemporary women.

Korean women's poetry dates back as far as the ancient Korea of the Old Chosŏn period (TRAD. 2333 B.C.E.). One of the first poems of Korea, "Konghuin," is known to have been composed and sung by a woman called Yŏok. Kim Hyesoon notes that since Korean women have had a marginal status in Korean society, women's literary traditions are rooted in oral literature, such as the ancient songs (*kodae kayo*) of Old Chosŏn, and the poem-songs (*hyangga*) that displayed the native spirituality and Buddhist faith of the Three Kingdoms period and Unified Silla (TRAD. 57 B.C.E.-936 C.E.).

In the Koryŏ period (918-1392 C.E.) the only written record of women's poetry has been left by *kisaeng*, female entertainers who were outcasts. During this period Chinese characters and classical Chinese literature were adopted by the ruling class and became the dominant form of literature. Therefore, women's poetry came to exist primarily within Koryŏ's rich oral tradition (*Koryŏ sogyo*) that mostly consisted of poem-songs (*siga* or *kayŏ*). Further subordination of oral literature occurred in the subsequent Chosŏn period (1392-1910 C.E.), as the ruling class idealized and adopted neo-Confucian philosophy and classical Chinese literary traditions. Women lived under strict patriarchal and hierarchical neo-Confucian values that demanded the strict division of gender roles and spaces. But self-educated, upper-class (*yangban*) women wrote instructional letters/poem-songs (*kyubang kasa*) that were mainly passed down from women to women, mothers to daughters. These songs, usually recorded in *hangŭl*, spoke of family genealogy, proper conduct, women's duty and obedience to husbands, in-laws, parents, and, most importantly, women's laments of their sorrows and suffering. *Sijo,* a three-line lyric form that became widely practiced during this period, was originally written mostly by men of the ruling class, the upper class literati. The only women who engaged in the writing of *sijo* were *kisaeng*. Some of the writings in *hangŭl* by the privileged daughters of *yangban* families were rewritten in Chinese by their brothers and recorded in their collection of poems or prose. The pre-modern Korean women's literature that Kim Hyesoon most identifies with is *muga,* songs of shaman, because in these narratives, women display an awareness of their social conditions and redefine their identity. And because of the long history and achievement within women's literary tradition, Kim believes that "poetry is the best location from which Korean women can speak," despite the fact that women's poetry is still pushed to the margins within Korea's male-dominated poetry world.

By the early 1900s, Korean women poets and prose writers began to publish their work publicly for the first time. The women who received a modern education in the early 1900s, contemporaries to the national struggle, were referred to as the "new women" (*sinyŏsŏng*). The pioneer "new women" poets of modern Korea in the 1920s were

Kim Myŏng-sun (1896-1951), Na Hye-sŏk (1896-1946), and Kim Wŏn-ju (1896-1971) who, like many intellectuals of the colonial era, were also educated in Japan. They advocated for sexual freedom, gender equality, and women's liberation from patriarchal institutions such as arranged marriages, polygamy, and prostitution. Such feminist consciousness did not reemerge until the poets of the 1970s, Mun and Kang, and the three poets represented in this anthology.

In the 1930s, *yŏryu* (female) poetry used gentle and refined language to speak about women's passivity. Two prominent women poets of the 1930s, Mo Yun-suk (1910-1990) and No Ch'ŏn-myŏng (1912-1957) helped define *yŏryu* poetry, and their work represents the "twin walls," or the two dominant trends, in modern Korean women's poetry. Mo's work contains highly emotional tendencies, while No's work is considered to be more reflective and emotionally restrained, which helped to gain it wide acceptance among the male modernist poets of the time. No's work is still cherished and respected by Korea's literary establishment while Mo's is less highly regarded because of her emotionalism and lesser literary sophistication. The *yŏryu siin* (a female poet) was expected to write "sentimental" and "gentle" poetry—like Mo and No. This term *yŏryu siin* is still widely used in Korea to refer to female poets, while men are referred to as *siin*—"poet."

The poetry of Ch'oe Sŭng-ja, Kim Hyesoon, and Yi Yŏn-ju violates the literary expectations of *yŏryu* (female) poetry through their innovative language and depictions of Korean women's identities, lives, and struggles. These poets also resist the enormous pressure to conform to mainstream lyrical poetry, which is deeply rooted in the tradition of Korean poetry written in classical Chinese, expressing tranquil and transcendental nature. Ch'oe employs one of the common literary devices of contemporary Korean women poets, which Kim Hyesoon refers to as a "confessional device" that opposes and resists her outside world—specifically the patriarchy. Kim employs a "conversational device" that involves the use of conversations between multiple selves within a woman to discover her own identity. Yi, like Ch'oe, starkly and powerfully embraced the language of decay and death. Yi's literary device, according to Kim, is a "diary-like" type of documentation that resists universalizing metaphors.

The three poets also defy the traditional gender roles that persist today by publicly participating in literary production and by refusing to fall into the roles of *ch'ŏnyŏ* (a young unmarried woman/virgin), *ajumma* (married woman/middle aged woman with children) and *halmŏni* (grandmother). In pre-modern Korea, the only women who publicly produced poetry, as part of their work, were *kisaeng*, the outcast entertainers.

Ch'oe, Kim, and Yi have challenged both literary and gender expectations, and, in South Korea's highly patriarchal and structured society, created groundbreaking, provocative poetry that insists on remaining outside the mainstream.

Their poetry from the margins continues to play a critical role in the development of contemporary Korean women's poetry. Kim Hyesoon points out that since the 1990s, feminist poets have "opposed all oppression," in particular by internalizing or encoding the revolutionary and political intent of the poetry of the 1980s into their poetic language. More women poets have begun to write about their newly discovered female identities and realities that previously had been suppressed and unexplored. The resulting poetry is aptly described by Kim Sŭng-hŭi, a contemporary and colleague of Kim Hyesoon, in her book of criticism, *Men Do Not Know* (*Namjadŭrŭn morŭnda*, 2001): A literature of laughter./ A literature of white breast-milk./ A literature of rifts./ A literature of abomination.

* * *

I owe deep gratitude to friends, colleagues, and teachers who have generously offered their support and inspiration: Bruce and Ju-Chan Fulton modeled for me persistence without which I could not have envisioned this book. My very first publication of my translations in *Arts & Letters* was made possible by E. Ethelbert Miller. Minnie Bruce Pratt gave me unwavering confidence and critical insights that sustained me. Margo Okazawa-Rey and Gwyn Kirk exposed me to the agency of women in South Korea. Deborah Woodard read every translation and offered editorial assistance through which I learned to be a better translator. Yi Yong-ju generously shared biographical information about his sister, Yi. Kim and Ch'oe offered me their knowledge of contemporary Korean women's poetry. A brief, unexpected encounter with Steven Bradbury in 2004 led me to Zephyr Press. Cris Mattison's sensitive editing gave more power to the voices of Ch'oe, Kim, and Yi. Finally, I dedicate this book to my parents who took many risks in order to pave a path for me.

—*Don Mee Choi*

최승자

Ch'oe Sŭng-ja

Ch'oe Sŭng-ja (b.1952) is one of the most highly regarded contemporary women poets of South Korea. She spent part of her early childhood in Yŏngi, a small rural town in Southern Ch'ungch'ŏn province, and then moved to Seoul with her family where she grew up. Ch'oe studied German literature at Korea University at a time when there were only two hundred women enrolled in the entire school. She began writing poetry while in college and became the first woman editor of Korea University's literary journal. In 1979, Ch'oe became the first woman poet to be published in a literary journal, *Literature and Intellect* (*Munhak kwa jisŏng*). This journal, along with *Creation and Criticism* (*Ch'angjak kwa pip'yŏng*), were the two leaders of the intellectual and literary movement against the U.S.-backed military dictatorships of Park Chung Hee and Chun Doo Hwan in the 1970s and 80s.

Ch'oe's poetry, which violated the criteria of decorum that had been long imposed on women poets, caused a stir in South Korea's predominantly male literary establishment. Her language and subject matter were attacked for being too rough and vulgar for a "female poet" (*yŏryu siin*). Despite the harsh criticisms leveled against her work, Ch'oe remained active in literary circles, engaging in lively literary public and private debates. Ch'oe is part of the new wave of feminist poets of Korea to emerge after the early pioneering women poets of the 1920s such as Kim Myŏng-sun and Kim Wŏn-ju, who explored and gave voice to women's lives under the oppressive patriarchy.

Ch'oe published four collections of poetry between 1981 and 1993. In 1994, she participated in the Iowa International Writers' Program. By the late 1990s, Ch'oe had fallen into a deep spiritual malaise. Her spiritual search spurred her into constant movement, and, for a year or two, she traveled all over South Korea. She eventually fell ill, a condition that lasted for several years. After a long hiatus, Ch'oe reemerged with a book of poems called *Lovers* (*Yŏnintŭl*) in 2001. She now works as a literary translator in Seoul, where she is currently translating a collection of short stories by J.D. Salinger.

The poems in translation are selected from Ch'oe's second collection of poems, *Happy Diary* (*Chŭlgŏun ilgi*, 1984).

197x 년의 우리들의 사랑

—아무도 그 시간의 火傷 을 지우지 못했다

몇 년 전, 제기동 거리엔 건조한 먼지들만 횡행했고 우리는 언제나 우리가 아니었다. 우리는 언제나 잠들어 있거나 취해 있거나 아니면 시궁창에 빠진 헤진 신발짝처럼 더러운 물결을 따라 하염없이 흘러가고 있었고.... 제대하여 복학한 늙은 학생들은 아무 여자하고나 장가가 버리고 사학년 계집아이들은 아무 남자하고나 약혼해 버리고 착한 아이들은 알맞는 향기를 내뿜으며 시들어 갔다.

그해 늦가을과 초겨울 사이, 우리의 노쇠한 혈관을 타고 그리움의 피는 흘렀다. 그리움의 어머니는 마른 강줄기, 술과 불이 우리를 불렀다. 향유 고래 울음 소리 같은 밤 기적이 울려 퍼지고 개처럼 우리는 제기동 빈 거리를 헤맸다. 눈알을 한없이 굴리면서 꿈속에서도 행진해 나갔다. 때로 골목마다에서 진짜 개들이 기총소사하듯 짖어대곤 했다. 그러나 197x년, 우리들 꿈의 오합지졸들이 제아무리 집중 사격을 가해도 현실은 요지부동이었다. 우리의 총알은 언제나 절망만으로 만들어진 것이었으므로 ...

어느덧 방학이 오고 잠이 오고 깊은 눈이 왔을 때 제기동 거리는 "미안해, 사랑해" 라는 말로 진흙탕을 이루었고 우리는 잠 속에서도 "사랑해, 죽여 줘" 라는 잠꼬대를 했고 그때마다 마른번개 사이로 그리움의 어머니는 야윈 팔을 치켜들고 나직이 말씀하셨다. "세상의 아들아 내 손이 비었구나, 너희에게 줄 게 아무것도 없구나." 그리고 우리는 정말로 개처럼 납작하게 엎드려 고요히 침을 흘리며 죽어갔다.

Our Love of 197x

— No one has been able to salve the burn of that hour

Several years ago, only dust blew over the streets of Chegidong and we were not ourselves. We were always asleep or drunk or following a filthy tide, forever drifting away like a torn shoe fallen into a ditch.... The older male students would marry just any woman when they returned to school after finishing compulsory military service, and the fourth-year female students would get engaged to just any man, and the good young people faded away, giving off just the right scent.

That late fall and early winter, the blood of longing flowed in our decrepit veins. The mother of longing was a dried up river. Fire and wine called to us. An evening whistle rippled across like the cry of a sperm whale as we roamed the empty streets of Chegidong like dogs. We rolled our eyes endlessly and marched forward even in our dreams. At times, real dogs barked like machine guns from each alley. However, in 197x, reality remained steadfast even though the mobs in our dreams carried out an armed assault. Because our bullets were made only of despair …

Somehow, when the school break came, when sleep came, when the deep snow came, the streets of Chekidong grew muddy, saying "Sorry, I love you." We even talked in our sleep and every time we cried, "I love you, please kill me," the Mother of longing raised her thin arms and spoke softly, "Son of the world, my hand is empty. I have nothing to give you." Then we lay flat, dying, drooling silently like real dogs.

내가 너를 너라고 부를 수 없는 곳에서

1.

어느 한 순간 세계의 모든 음모가
한꺼번에 불타오르고
우연히 발을 잘못 디딜 때
터지는 지뢰처럼
꿈도 도처에서 폭발한다

삼억 이천만 원짜리 선글래스를 낀 것은 그젯밤의 꿈,

어두운 밝음 속에서
우리가 서로를 껴안은 것은
어젯밤의 꿈,

네가 떠나고
바람 불고
내가 죽는 것은
오늘 한낮의 꿈.

2.

또다시 한 세월이 끝났을 때
나의 무릎은 절단되어 있었고
너의 문은 닫혀 있었다.

네가 없는 그 거리,
나침판이, 운명 지침서가 헛돌고
한 평생이, 온 인류가 헛돌고

헛도는 그 깊이로
흩어져 내리는 내 꽁지의
마지막 깃털이 보였다.

6

From a Place Where I Can't Call You as You

1.

All at once the world's game plan is on fire,
and the dream explodes like when,
by chance, you step on a land mine.

Wearing those 320 million *won* sunglasses is the previous night's dream.

Embracing each other
inside a blazing darkness
is last night's dream.

You leave,
a wind blows,
I die.
Today's dream of daylight.

2.

Once again as time elapsed
my knees were cut,
your door was shut.

The street where you are no longer
a compass, fate's needle spins
a lifetime, all humanity spins needlessly.

Within the depth of the spin,
the falling of final
tail feathers grows visible.

3.

내가 너를 너라고 부를 수 없는 곳에서
흐르는 물은 흐름을 정지하고

이제 눈 감는 자는 영원히
다시 눈 떠 헤매지 않으리니

말없이 한 여자가 떠나가고
바다의 회색 철문이 닫혀진다.

3.

From a place where I can't call you as you
I stop the stream of flowing water.

Now the one whose eyes close
will never open them again to seek.

One woman leaves wordlessly,
and the sea's gray steel door shuts.

나날

눈알을 앞으로 달고 있어도
눈알을 뒤로 바꾸어 달아도
약속된 비젼은 나타나지 않고

창가의 별이 쉬임없이 늙어 간다.
치아 끝이 자꾸 바스러져 나간다.
날마다 신부들은 무덤으로 떠나가고
날마다 앞 못 보는 아기들이 한 트럭씩 태어나고
느리고 더딘 미끄러짐이 시작된다.

어둠의 볼륨을 좀 더 높여라.
날마다의 커피에 증오의 독을 조금씩 더 치고
그래 그래 치정처럼 집요하게 우리는
죽음의 확실한 모습을 기다리고

그러나 냉동된 달빛 뚝뚝 떨어져 꽂히고
벽시계 과앙과앙 울리고
스틱을 든 불길한 검은 신사가
마지막 문간에 나타날 때
우리는 허리 짤린 개미떼처럼 황급히 흩어져
습기찬 잠의 굴 속으로 기어내려간다.

Every Day

Whether the eyeballs get hung to the front,
whether the eyeballs get moved to the rear,
the promised enigma doesn't appear.

Stars by the window age endlessly,
the tooth's edge crumbles,
every day brides retreat to the grave,
every day blind infants are born by the truckload,
so begins a slow, tedious slide.

Turn up the volume of darkness.
Spoon the poison of rage bit by bit into daily coffee.
Right, right, like a stubborn blind love,
we wait for death to zero in.

But as the frozen moonlight drops like arrows,
the clock's chimes echo,
and the ominous dark gentleman holding a stick
appears at the final gate;
we scatter like ants severed at the waist
and crawl into the damp cave of sleep.

연습

한잠 자고 일어나 보면
당신은 먼 태양 뒤로 숨어 보이지 않는다.
이윽고 어 얼마 뒤, 불편한 안개 뒷편으로
당신은 어 엉거주춤 떠오르기 시작한다,
이상하게, 낯설게,
시체 나라의 태양처럼 차갑게.
나는 그 낯설고 차가운 열기에
온몸을 찔리며 포복한 채
당신에게로 기어가기 시작한다.
이윽고 거북스런 안개가 걷히고
당신과 나는 당당하게 서로를 바라본다.

그때 당신이 또 날 죽이려는 음모를 품기 시작한다.
뒤에다 무엇인가를 숨기고서
당신은 꿀물을 타 주면 자꾸만 마시라고 한다.
나는 그게 독물인 줄 알면서도 자꾸만 받아 마신다.
나는 내 두 발이 빠져 들어가는 것을 알면서도
자꾸만 빠져 들어간다.
당신은 당신이 하는 장난이
내게는 얼마나 무서운 진실인가를 모르는 체한다.

당신이 모르는 체하는 것을 모르는 체하면서,
내가 자꾸 빠져 들어가는 게 나의 사랑이라는 것을 당신은
모르고, 모르는 체하고,
그리고 보이지 않는 곳에서 진딧물이 벼룩을 낳고 벼룩이
바퀴벌레를 낳고 바퀴벌레가 거미를 낳고 …
우리의 사랑도 속수무책 거미줄만 깊어 가고,
또 다른 해가 차가운 구덩이에 처박힌다.

A Practice

After I rise from a long sleep
you cannot be seen,
for you've hidden behind the distant sun.
Soon after, you hover and rise behind
the uneasy fog, as mysteriously
as a cold sun up from the dead.
Stabbed and cowed by the unfamiliar, frigid heat
I crawl toward you.
At last, the fog lifts;
you and I boldly stare at each other.

You start to plot to kill me again.
You hide something behind your back
and insist that I drink the honeyed water you're offering.
I keep accepting and drinking, knowing it's poisoned.
Knowing my feet are sinking, slipping down through.
You deny that the game you're playing is a terrifying reality to me.

I deny your denial;
you are ignorant, you ignore
that my endless sinking is this love of mine,
and from a hidden place,
an aphid gives birth to a flea, the flea gives birth to a roach
and the roach gives birth to a spider …
Our love like a helpless cobweb deepens,
and another sun is kicked into a cold pit.

끊임없이 나를 찾는 전화 벨이 울리고

많은 사람들이 흘러갔다
욕망과 욕망의 찌꺼기인 슬픔을 등에 얹고
그들은 나의 창가를 스쳐 흘러갔다.
나는 흘러가지 않았다.

나는 흘러가지 않았다.
열망과 허망을 버무려
나는 하루를 생산했고
일년을 생산했고
죽음의 월부금을 꼬박꼬박 지불했다.

그래, 끊임없이 나를 호출하는 전화 벨이 울리고
나는 피해 가고 싶지 않았다.
그 구덩이에 내가 함몰된다 하더라도
나는 만져 보고 싶었다,
운명이여.

그러나 또한 끊임없이 나는 문을 닫아 걸었고
귀와 눈을 닫아 걸었다.
나는 철저한 조건반사의 기계가 되어
아침엔 밥을 부르고
저녁엔 잠을 쑤셔 넣었다.

궁창의 빈터에서 거대한 허무의 기계를 가동시키는
하늘의 키잡이 늙은 니힐리스트여,
당신인가 나인가
누가 먼저 지칠 것인가
(물론 나는 그 결과를 알고 있다.
내가 당신을 창조했다는 것까지)

끊임없이 나를 찾는 전화 벨이 울리고
그 전화선의 마지막 끝에 동굴 같은
썩은 늪 같은 당신의 口腔이 걸려 있었다.
어느 날 그곳으로부터 죽음은
결정적으로 나를 호명할 것이고
나는 거기에 결정적으로 응답하리라.

The Phone Rings Endlessly

Many people drifted away
past my window, carrying
desire and sadness on their backs, desire's leftovers.
I didn't drift away.

I didn't drift away.
I mixed zeal and nothingness
and produced a day,
produced a year,
and faithfully paid monthly installments on death.

That's right, the phone rings endlessly.
I didn't want to avoid it.
Destiny, I wanted to touch it
even though I might sink into its pit.

But, at the same time, I locked my door,
locked my ears and eyes forever.
I became robotic to the core.
I shouted for rice in the morning
and shoved in sleep at night.

An aging nihilist, a giant of the sky
operates a great machine of nothingness in heaven's empty space.
Who will tire first?
You or me?
(Of course, I know the outcome.
Also the fact that I created you.)

The phone rings endlessly.
At the end of the line your mouth hung
like a cave, like a decayed bog.
From there, death will decisively
call my name some day,
and I'll answer.

타들어가는 내 운명의 도화선이
당신의 썩은 口腔 안에서 폭발하리라.
삼십 년 전부터 다만 헛되이,
헛되고 헛됨을 완성하기 위하여.

늙은 니힐리스트, 당신은 피묻은 너털웃음을 한번 날리고
그 노후의 몸으로 또다시 고요히
허무의 기계를 돌리기 시작하리라.
몇 천 년 전부터 다만 헛되이,
헛되고 헛됨을 다 이루었다고 말하기 위하여.

My destiny's burning fuse
will explode inside your rotten mouth
to perfect the past thirty years of
futile, idle, futility.

Aging nihilist, you'll let out a bloodied boisterous laugh,
then with your aged body, you'll silently
start the machine of nothingness again
to say you have completed
the past several thousand years of
futile, idle, futility.

폰 가갸 씨의 肖像

9시, 사무실 출입문이 폰 가갸 씨를 기운차게 연다.
의자가 걸어와 폰 가갸 씨 위에 앉는다.
볼펜이 그의 손가락을 꼬나쥐고
활자들이 그를 꼬나보기 시작한다.

12시, 점심이 그를 잘도 먹어 치우고
때가 되면 오줌이 유유하게 그를 갈긴다.
때때로 심심해서 전화가 자꾸 그를 걸어 본다.
여보십니까? 여보십니다! (존재의 딸꾹질)
시간이 가기도 하고 안 가기도 하면서
이윽고 월급 봉투가 그를 호주머니에 쑤셔 넣는다.
6시 반, 54번 버스가 다시 폰 가갸 씨를 올라탄다.
원효대교가 다시 홀라당 그를 넘어간다.

현관문이 그를 열고 집어 넣는다.
따뜻한 방바닥이 그를 때려눕힌다.
잠이 아작아작 그를 갉아먹기 시작한다.
그러나 이윽고!
꿈 속에서 대한민국이 열렬하게 그를 찬양하고
여의도 광장 한가운데에 그의 기념비를 세운다.
코러스도 웅장하게 울려 퍼지며
우러러 찬미할지어다!

Portrait of von Ka-kya

9 AM, the office door bursts open with von Ka-kya.
A chair walks over and sits on von Ka-kya.
A pen holds on to the end his fingers,
and the letters stare angrily at him.

12 PM, lunch finishes him up;
when it's time, urine calmly pees on him.
Often, out of boredom, the phone keeps calling him.
Are you, hello? I'm, hello! (A hiccup of an existence.)
Time stops and goes.
Finally the paycheck stuffs him into a pocket.
6:30 PM, bus number 54 gets on von Ka-kya again.
Again the Wŏnhyo Bridge runs over him.

The front door opens and shoves him in.
The heated floor beats him down.
Sleep begins to chew on him, crunch crunch.
But after a while
in his dream, the Republic of Korea praises him passionately
and places a statue of him in the middle of Yŏŭi Island's public square.
The chorus ripples magnificently.
Praise, praise!

여의도 광시곡

1.

가물거리는 정신의 한 끝을 헤집고 나와
다시 다른 한 끝에서 침몰하기 위하여
원효대교, 그 허상의 다리를 넘어
섬으로 진입하는 사람들.
유해 색소의 햇빛에 조금씩 들끓으며
발효하기 시작하는 거대한 반죽 덩어리.

> —여의도는 거룩한
> 天上의 빵

2.

구르는 헛바퀴의 완강한 힘, 치욕이여
중국집 짬뽕 속의 삶은 바퀴벌레여,
그래도 코를 벌름거리며
돼지들은 죽어서도 즐겁고
오, 제 먹는 게 제 살인 줄 모르는
무의식의 죄의식의 내출혈의 비몽사몽의

> 손들엇 탕탕!
> 창밖엔 찌를 듯 환한 햇빛
> 샛강 빈 벌판에서, 누가 노래 불러?
> 귀아리게
> 쟁쟁하게
> 불끈 솟아오르는 산들,
> 어린 날의 메아리가 되살아나
> 흐야 호 바다로 내달아
> 바다!
> 일어나!
> 솟구쳐!
> 위로
> 위로
> 정점의 피
> 태양

Yŏŭi Island: A Rhapsody

1.

They come out tearing one end of a flickering consciousness
in order to attack the other;
people cross the phantom legs of the Wŏnhyo Bridge
and parade onto the island.
In the sunlight of noxious pigments
the massive lump of dough
bubbles up bit by bit,
begins to ferment.
                    — Yŏŭi Island is the divine heaven's bread

2.

The persistent power of a senseless spinning wheel, the disgrace;
the roach boiled inside Chinese noodle soup,
even the pigs' noses quiver,
and the pigs remain happy despite being dead.
Oh! Not knowing what it's eating is its own flesh,
the unconscious of conscience of hemorrhage of trance.

                                    Hands up! Bang bang!
                        The jabbing sunlight outside a window.
                                    The piercing voice,
                                        ear biting.
                    Who is singing in the vacant field by the river?
                            The sudden rising of mountains.
                        The echoes of a childhood come alive,
                                Ya ho! Run to the sea. Sea!
                                                Sea!
                                        Get up!
                            Shoot up!
                    Up
            Up
    Summit's blood
    Sun

3.

그러나 예, 기다려야지요.
즐거운 사탕발림의 기다림.
그러나 예, 기다려야지요.
우리의 기다림에도
프리미엄이 붙을 테니까요.

오 이 느긋한 기다림의 사원에서
영원히 기다리게 하소서.
마지막 임종처럼 다가올
약속의 땅을 꿈꾸며
우리 네 활개 펴고
잠들어 있게 하소서,
지금 여기서 영원히.

4.

시간은 저 혼자 능률 능률 흘러가고
보라, 우리의 오물더미 위에서,
구린내도 그윽한 문화의 오븐 위에서
무럭무럭 김을 풍기며
거대하게 부풀어 오르는 여의도를.
　　　　　　　　　　　　—여의도는 거대한
　　　　　　　　　　　　　　天上의 빵

그윽한 향취 속에서
저는 잠든 것도 깬 것도 아니었어요.
다만 이 세상을 손수건처럼 얌전히 접어 두고서
한 세월 아득히 눕고 싶었을 뿐이에요.
—그때 거기에서 많은 사람들이 울고 있었는데
　나는 왜? 알지 못했죠.
—그때 그 거리에서 검은 상복 입은 사람들이
　바다로 내닫고 있었는데
　나는 왜? 알지 못했죠.

3.

Yes, however, we must wait.
The joyous wait for the pleasure of sweets.
Yes, however, we must wait
because as we wait
the premium grows.

Oh! Please let us wait endlessly
in this marvelous temple of waiting.
Please let us dream of the promised land
that draws near like the final hour of death,
and please let us stay asleep with
our four limbs spread apart
now, here, forever.

4.

Time drifts punctually by itself.
Look, the island swells up immense
on top of our garbage dump;
the stench mushrooms
above the profound culture's oven.

— Yŏŭi Island is the vast heaven's bread

Within the profound fragrance
I'm not awake not asleep,
just keeping this world neatly folded like a handkerchief
and wishing that I could lie alone for a while.
  — That time when many people cried over there,
    why didn't I know?
  — That time when people in the streets,
    wearing dark funeral outfits, dashed off to the sea,
    why didn't I know?

하지만 어느 순간 내 꿈을 타고 한 마리 뱀이
내 입 속으로 목구멍 속으로 들어가고
그 순간 큰골이 팽팽한 풍선처럼
내 머리 밖으로 부풀어오르고

그때 나는 보았죠.
피골이 상접한 내 정신이
땡땡 부어오른 내 육신의 관을 이끌고
대방 터널을 힘겹게 빠져 나가는 것을.

5.

날개 돋힌 듯 홰를 치며
열심히 빵을 굽는 사람들
살인적으로 미소짓는 假花들
심장과 성기와 항문을 발랑
얼굴에 달고 다니는 사람들

혹은 삶 속에 죽음의 기념비를 세우며
심장과 성기와 항문을 꼭꼭 잠그고
막대그래프처럼 걷는 사람들
차트 같은 표정의 얼굴들

옛날의 금잔디
창가에서 노래하던
처녀들의 순한 목소리 문득 그치고
수직으로 곧게 추락하는 새들.
보이지 않게 습한 기류의 이동이 시작되고
비닐조각 볼펜 서류철,
인기 가수의 사진들, 사산된 아이들이
검은 하구로 떠내려와
검은 운명을 짜맞추기 시작한다.
—각성하라
  너희의 꿈을 뒤덮을
  홍수가 진행되고 있다.
  그리고 너희에겐 되돌아갈 땅,
  세습의 땅도 없다.

At a certain moment, a snake
climbs up my dream and into my mouth, into my throat,
just then the cerebrum puffs up outside
my head like an overblown balloon.

I saw it then,
my consciousness, skin and bone, pulling
the inflated coffin of my body,
struggling to slip out from the tunnel of feces.

5.

People bake bread diligently,
flapping their sprouted wings.
People go around with
murderously smiling fake flower
hearts and genitals and anuses
hung on their faces.

Sometimes people set up a monument
of remembrance for death within life,
tightly closed hearts and genitals and anuses
and walk like bars from a graph
with blank expressions on their faces.

Young women singing
Golden grass of the old days
by the window
suddenly silence their innocent voices,
and birds plunge perpendicular to the ground.
The invisible movement of humid air currents begins.
Bits of plastic bags, pens, files,
photos of a popular singer, shattered children
float down to the river's dark mouth
and begin to fabricate a dark fate.
     — Wake up!
     The flood that will cover up your dreams heads out.
     There is no land for you to return to, not even ancestral land.

6.

지렁이들도 꾸물꾸물 꿈을 꾸기 시작하고
네온사인의 젖은 미소 피어 오르고
地下의 死者들도 감겼던 눈을
일제히 치켜뜨고 地上을 응시하는,
거두절미하고, 밤이 온다.
반신불수의 밤, 그러나 영혼불면의 밤.
반짝이는 눈을 가진 쥐새끼들은
포식의 탁자 위에서 공영 방송과
분 냄새 나는 잡지들과 주식회사
경영 방침을 논의하며
한 사회의 아마도 광대한 몇 바퀴의 헛바퀴와
한 개인의 아마도 무수한 개미 쳇바퀴가
여전히 맞물려 돌아가면서
잘 구도된, 또 하나의 완벽한
폐허를 향해 전진해 가고,

여의도는 뒤로 벌렁 누운
거대한 다족류의 벌레.
그 무수한 발끝마다 네온사인을 달고
허공을 향해 수만 개의 발가락을 꼬물거리면서
입으로는 하루종일 먹었던 온갖 더러움을
게거품처럼 조용히 게워내고

여의도 허공 가장 깊숙한 곳에선
神의 형상을 한 거대한 검은 아가리가
이 세계의 남은 뼈를 아득아득 씹고 있다.

        —여의도는 거룩한
           天上의 빵

6.

Worms start to dream wiggle wiggle,
wet smiles of neon signs bloom;
all at once the dead of the underground
open their shut eyes and gaze at the surface.
Severed heads and tails
as night arrives.
A night of split paralysis but a night of souls' immortality.
Rats with twinkling eyes
on a table of gluttony
debate with public broadcasts and magazines scented with cosmetics
about a finance group's management policies.
In gear as always
maybe the immense senseless wheels among wheels of one society,
and maybe the countless go rounds in circles of one individual
spin
as they charge towards
one more well designed, perfect ruin.

Yŏŭi Island, nimbly lying on its back,
is a great millipede.
Neon signs attached to the end of its numerous feet,
it wiggles thousands of its toes towards the air;
its mouth that all day long has eaten every kind of filth
quietly spits it out like a crab's froth.

In the deepest part of Yŏŭi Island's vacuous space,
the dark gigantic mouth takes on the shape of God
and chews crunch crunch on the remaining bones of this world.
　　　　　　　　　　　　　— Yŏŭi Island is the divine heaven's bread

그리하여 어느 날, 사랑이여

한 숟갈의 밥, 한 방울의 눈물로
무엇을 채울 것인가,
밥을 눈물에 말아먹는다 한들.

그대가 아무리 나를 사랑한다 해도
혹은 내가 아무리 그대를 사랑한다 해도
나는 오늘의 닭고기를 씹어야 하고
나는 오늘의 눈물을 삼켜야 한다.
그러므로 이젠 비유로써 말하지 말자.
모든 것은 콘크리트처럼 구체적이고
모든 것은 콘크리트 벽이다.
비유가 아니라 주먹이며,
주먹의 바스라짐이 있을 뿐,

이제 이룰 수 없는 것을 또한 이루려 하지 말며
헛대고 헛됨을 이루었도다고도 말하지 말며

가거라, 사랑인지 사람인지,
사랑한다는 것은 너를 위해 죽는 게 아니다.
사랑한다는 것은 너를 위해
살아,
기다리는 것이다,
다만 무참히 꺾여지기 위하여.

그리하여 어느 날 사랑이여,
내 몸을 분질러다오.
내 팔과 다리를 꺾어

네

꽃
병
에

꽂
아
다
오

So One Day, Love …

A spoonful of rice, a falling tear,
What can they fill
even if the tear were to be eaten with rice?

No matter how much you say you love me,
no matter how much I say I love you,
I still need to chew today's chicken
and swallow today's tears.
So let's not speak metaphorically.
Everything is tangible as concrete,
everything is a concrete wall.
Not a metaphor but a fist;
there's only the crushing fist.

Now, don't try to attain the unattainable,
don't talk about what's useless, the futility already attained.

Go, whether you are human or Love.
To love doesn't mean that I should die for you.
To love means that I should live for you and wait
for the ruthless break.

So one day, Love,
destroy my body,
break off my arms and legs
and
arrange
them
in
your
flower
vase.

K를 위하여

허물처럼 벗어던진 브래지어가
나무 의자 등어리에 걸려 있고
사랑은 나가 몇 달째 돌아오지 않는다.
부정한 아내야,
슬픔의 매독균을 간직한 여자야,
네가 가는 곳 그 어디마다
후광 같은 피고름의 응어리가 빛나누나.

에잇 돌아가자 돌아가자
안 넘어가는 사랑은
열 번을 찍어도 안 넘어가고
돌아가자 돌아가자
해 저물고 배고프고
피 팔아 술 마시고
우흐흐하 돌아가자
돌아간다 돌아간다
도라간다도라간다도라간다
에잇,
돌아와라 이년!
밤마다 빈 허공을 찍는 내 도끼날이 안 보이느냐?

For K

A bra discarded like skin
hangs from the back of a chair,
and love that had left has not returned for months.
You, a dishonest wife,
keeper of a virus of sorrow,
everywhere you go
the core of pus glows
like a halo.

Damn, let's go back, go back.
Love that can't be attained
can't be fulfilled no matter
how many times you try.
Let's go back, go back.
The sun's setting.
I'm hungry;
will sell blood for wine.
Wowhahaha! Let's go back,
go back, go back,
gobackgobackgoback.
Damn, come back, bitch!
Can't you see the blade of my ax striking a hollow spot each night?

Y 를 위하여

너는 날 버렸지,
이젠 헤어지자고
너는 날 버렸지,
산 속에서 바닷가에서
나는 날 버렸지.

수술대 위에 다리를 벌리고 누웠을 때
시멘트 지붕을 뚫고 하늘이 보이고
날아가는 새들의 폐벽에 가득찬 공기도 보였어.

하나 둘 셋 넷 다섯도 못 넘기고
지붕도 하늘도 새도 보이잖고
그러나 난 죽으면서 보았어.
나와 내 아이가 이 도시의 시궁창 속으로 시궁창 속으로
세월의 자궁 속으로 한없이 흘러가던 것을.
그때부터야.
나는 이 지상에 한 무덤으로 누워 하늘을 바라고
나의 아이는 하늘을 날아다닌다.
올챙이꼬리 같은 지느러미를 달고.
       나쁜 놈, 난 널 죽여 버리고 말 거야
        널 내 속에서 다시 낳고야 말 거야
내 아이는 드센 바람에 불려 지상에 떨어지면
내 무덤 속에서 몇 달간 따스하게 지내다
또다시 떠나가지 저 차가운 하늘 바다로,
올챙이꼬리 같은 지느러미를 달고.
오 개새끼
못 잊어!

For Y

You abandoned me.
You wanted us to part
you abandoned me.
On the mountain, at sea,
I abandoned me.

As I lay with my legs spread apart on the operating table,
my eyes broke through the cement roof and saw the sky.
I also saw the air filled up inside the flying birds' lungs.

I couldn't get beyond one, two, three, four, five.
I couldn't see the roof, sky, birds,
But I saw as I was dying
my child and I floating away into this city's
ditch, into the ditch, into time's vagina.

Since then
I lie in a grave and long for the sky,
and my child flies around
with a fin like a tadpole's tail attached.
        Wicked bastard, I'll kill you.
        I'll give birth to you inside me.
When my child gets blown down to the ground by a powerful wind,
spends a few months warm inside my grave
then floats away again to the cold sky sea
with a fin like a tadpole's tail attached.
Oh, son of a bitch!
Can't forget you!

告白

토해놓은 내장을 이젠 도로 삼키겠어요.
제자리에 다 삼키고서
이쁜 플라스틱 살로 가리겠어요.

이마와 양 뺨엔 박제된 눈물방울들을
구슬 장식처럼 은은히 달고서,
두 눈 감고 뿌리부터
몰래 몰래 썩기 시작하겠어요.

죽을 때까지 당신들을 교묘히 속이겠어요.
당신들이 안녕히 속을 수 있기만을 바랄 뿐예요.

속이고 또 속일 수 없는 어느 순간
거짓말처럼 가비얍게
내 일평생을 건너뛰어 버리겠어요.

(어쩌면 나의 외알 안경이
실수로 한 번쯤 눈물을 흘릴지도 모르지만.)

Confession

Puked intestines, I'll swallow them
right back down, after I swallow the lot.
I'll cover them with lovely plastic flesh.

On my forehead and cheeks, I hang
stuffed teardrops like delicate beads.
Close my two eyes and starting from the roots
I rot, rot quietly.

I'll cleverly deceive you until death.
My only wish is that all of you will be completely deceived.

The moment I can't deceive you again and again
like a fib I'll skip lightly over my entire life.

(My monocle may shed tears at least once by mistake.)

즐거운 일기

오늘 나는 기쁘다. 어머니는 건강하심이 증명되었고 밀린 번역료를 받았고 낮의 어느 모임에서 수수한 남자를 소개받았으므로.

오늘도 여의도 강변에선 날개들이 풍선돈친 듯 팔렸고 도곡동 개나리 아파트의 밤하늘에선 달님이 별님들을 둘러앉히고 맥주 한 잔씩 돌리며 봉봉 크랙카를 깨물고 잠든 기린이의 망막에선 노란 튤립꽃들이 까르르거리고 기린이 엄마의 꿈 속에선 포니 자가용이 휘발유도 없이 잘 나가고 피곤한 기린이 아빠의 겨드랑이에선 지금 남몰래 일 센티 미터의 날개가 돋고 …

수영이 삼촌 별아저씨 오늘도 캄사캄사합니다. 아저씨들이 우리 조카들을 많이많이 사랑해 주신 덕분에 오늘도 우리는 코리아의 유구한 푸른 하늘 아래 꿈 잘 꾸고 한판 잘 놀아났읍니다.

　　　아싸라비아
　　　도로아미타불

Happy Diary

Today I'm happy. Mother got a bill of good health and I finally received payment for a translation and was introduced to a modest looking man at an afternoon gathering.

Today on Yŏŭi Island's riverside, wings got sold like inflated balloons and in the night sky of Dokokdong's Forsythia Apartment, Moon sits Stars around and serves each a glass of beer and yellow tulips giggle on the vast plain of a sleeping Giraffe with a *Bong Bong* cracker still in its mouth and in the Giraffe's mom's dream, her very own *Pony* car drives smoothly without gasoline and in the armpit of Giraffe's dad a one centimeter wing sprouts secretly …

Uncle Star, Suyŏng's uncle, I thank you thank you for today. Because you uncles have loved our nephews so much, we were able to dream and play out a scandal under Korea's everlasting blue sky.

> *Assarabia*
> *Toroamit'abul*

無 題 2

1.

간밤 소리 없이 이슬 내린 뒤
현관 문이 가만히 울고
죽음은 우유 배달부의 길을 타고 온다.

누군가의 검은 눈빛,
늘어진 검은 손이
문고리를 부여잡고

순간, 거대한 그림자가
타이탄 트럭처럼 나를 덮치고
들렀다,
캄캄하게 낙락장송 쓰러지는 소리,
캄캄하게 한 시대가 길게 뻗는 소리.

2.

1983 년, 운명의 맞물림이 풀어지는 소리,
무한 궤도 속으로 떨어져 나가는 작은 객차 하나.
1983 년, 하나님은 경솔했고
나는 부실했다.
오 이 모든 진땀나는 공모! 공포!
이 세계를, 이 세계의 맨살의 공포를
나는 감당할 수 없다.
그러나 밀려온다,
이 세계는,
내 눈알의 깊은 망막을 향해
수십 억의 군화처럼 행군해 온다.

눈 감아요, 이제 곧 무서운 시간이 와요.
창자나 골수 같은 건 모두 쏟아 버려요.
토해 버려요, 한 시대의 썩은 음식물들을,
현실의 잠, 잠의 현실 속에서.
그리고 깊이깊이 가라앉아요.

Untitled 2

After last night's soundless mist
the front door cries out softly,
and death arrives, riding the milk man's path.

Someone's dark stare,
a dark limp hand
clutches a doorknob.

For a moment, a great shadow
falls on me like that of a Titan Truck, then lifts me;
the deep plunging sound of a magnificent pine tree,
the long dark stretch of an era.

2.

1983, the uncoiling sound of fate's encounter,
a tiny train falling into an infinite orbit.

In 1983, God did not heed,
and I was faithless.
Oh, the cold sweat of conspiracy! Terror!
I can't cope with this world, its naked terror.
But it closes in.
This world parades
like several million military boots
across my eye's deep retina.

Close your eyes, the hour of terror will soon arrive.
Discard things like intestines and brains.
Spit out the rotten food of an era
inside the sleep of reality, the reality of sleep.
Then sink down deep.

(고요히 한 세월의 밑바닥을 기어가며
나는 다족류의 벌레로 변해 갔다.)

　　　3.
이 시대 죽음의 잔은
이미 채워졌으니
네 몫은 필요치 않다.
그러니 가라!
어서 되돌아가라!

(한밤중에 문득 잠에서 깨어날 때
너희의 거울 속을 들여다보라.
거기, 이십 세기의 치욕인 내가
너희에게 은은한 치욕의 미소를 보내고 있을 것이다.)

만장하신 여러분
나를 죽이고 싶어 환장하신 여러분
오늘 내가 죽는 쇼는 이것으로 끝입니다.
십년 후 똑같은 시각에
똑같은 염통을 달고
이 장소로 나와 주십시요.

　　　4.
가을이 첫 국화송이를 맺을 때
어머니 한평생 미뤄 오던
한숨 피워 올리시고
표표히, 표표히 흩어지는 달무리.
살아 있는 자들은 그래도 하루의 양식을 즐길 것이며
살아 행복한 자들은 두번째 아이를 만들리니
설명할 수 없어 이 세계는 눕고
설명할 수 없어 이 세계의 길은 허공에 뜨고

한 체험의 파도의 깊이를 타고
한 채의 집이 금이 가
달빛만 받아도 기우뚱거리고,

(I turned into a millipede
as I crawled along the bottom of an era.)

3.

**Since the glass of this age's death
has already been filled,
your share is not needed,
so go!
Hurry, go back!**

(When you all awake suddenly
in the middle of the night,
look into your mirror.
From there, I, a disgrace to youth,
send you a faint smile of shame.)

Dear Ladies and Gentlemen,
You who are crazed by a wish to kill me,
this is the end of the show of my death.
Please come again
in ten years, at the same time,
wearing the same hearts.

4.

The moment autumn bears its first chrysanthemum,
Mother lets out the sigh she'd been repressing for a lifetime.
The ring around the moon shatters.
Those who are still alive will enjoy a day's meal.
Those who are happy and alive will make children for the second time.
The world lies down, for it can't explain.
Its path floats in the air, for it can't explain.

Ride the depth of an experience of a wave.
A house cracks even when it bathes in moonlight, it rocks.

들리누나, 오밤중엔 웬 거인이
온 세상에 교교하게 오줌 누는 소리.

(담 밖에서 나를 엿보는 자 있으니
필시 나의 다른 마음일지라*)

*이것은 나의 일년 신수풀이 중에 나오는 한 구절이다.

5.

어머니는 걸어가신다, 내 머릿속에서.
세상 한 켠을 고즈너기 울리며
어머니는 걸어가신다, 자꾸만 지구 반대편으로.
오래 걷고 오래 수고하며
해왕성을 지나 명왕성을 지나
쉬임 없이 내 꿈속을 걸어
마침내 어느 아침, 어머니는
내 문간에 당도하시리라.

그리고 이제 빛나지 않는 나날의 무덤 속에서
그러나 가능한 한 빛을 향해
한 아이가 태어날 준비를 서두르로 있다.
未明의 회색 창가에서.

문 밖에선 새벽 산길을 돌아온
그와 그의 마차가 나를 기다리고

멀리, 갇힌 수평선의 벽을 깨뜨리며
피 묻은 갈매기 한 마리가 탈출한다.

Hear the brilliant sound, a giant
urinating on the whole world at night.

(There is someone eyeing me from behind the wall.
Surely, it must be my other self.)

This is one of the phrases from my annual fortune

5.

Mother walks inside my head,
making one part of the world cry alone.
Mother keeps walking away from the earth.
She walks long and laboriously
past Neptune and Pluto,
walks endlessly in my dream,
and finally, one morning, Mother
arrives at my door.

And inside the grave of each dreary day
by the dimly lit window at dawn
a child hurriedly gets ready to be born
towards one possible light.

Outside my door
a man and his carriage wait for me
after their return from an early morning
outing on a mountain road.

A bloodied seagull breaks through the wall
of the horizon and flies off.

望祭

> 기도하십시요, 주여.
> 기도하십시요, 우리에게.
> 우리가 가까왔읍니다.
> —파울 첼란, 暗夜行 에서

봄에는 속이 환히 비치는 옷을 입고
일곱 송이의 꽃을 머리에 꽂고
마지막으로 신발을 벗어 버리고서,
청파동에서 수유리까지 손가락질하며
희죽거리며 걸어가고 싶다.
봄에는 황사처럼 아지랭이처럼 미쳐
수유리 하늘 끝에서
고요히 가물거리다 스러지고 싶다.

그러나 모든 까무러치지 못하는 사람들의 머리 위로
아찔한 한 시절이 가고 아득한 또 한 시절이 와,
남쪽 나라 바다 멀리 물새가 (안) 날고,
꽃잎은 하염없이 바람에 (안) 지고
이제 위로받아야 할 것은 우리,
무릎 꿇고 먼 세월을 기어가는 우리.

"우리 청춘의 유적지에선 아직도 비가 내린다더라.
그래서 멀리 누운 우리의 발가락에도
때로 빗물이 튀긴다고 하더라.
그리고 우리가 살아 있다는 헛소문이 간간이 들린다고도
하더라."

올 봄에도 하나님은 하늘의 궁창에 새를 심고 계시고
들판 식물들은 일시에 버혀짐으로써 향내를 풍기지만
당신들은 이제 진흙과 먼지로 돌아가려 하지 않는다.
보이지 않는 발목으로 그리운 옛 시가지를 헤매며
당신들은 살아 잠든 우리의 몸뚱어리를 노린다.

당신들을 무사히 물리쳐 버릴 수 있을까.
당신들을 무사히 죽음으로 되돌려보낼 수 있을까.
죽음과 삶이 상피붙는 神聖 코리아여

Prayers to Ancestor Spirits

Pray, Lord,
Pray, to us
We are near
　　　　　　　　　—Paul Celan, "Tenebrae"

In spring I want to put on a see-through dress,
wear seven flowers in my hair,
take off my shoes for the last time,
and walk, giggling and pointing my finger
from Ch'ŏngp'adong to Suyuri.
In spring I want to go crazy
like the shimmering haze, like the whirling sand
and flicker silently, then collapse
at the end of Suyuri's sky.

But above the heads of those forced to remain conscious,
a season of vertigo passes and another far away season arrives,
and waterfowl (don't) fly far across the sea to the lands of the south,
petals (don't) shed due to wind,
and it is we who need to be comforted.
We kneel and crawl toward a distant time.

"They say it still rains in the ruins of our youth.
So, they say at times rain splatters onto our distant corpses, our toes.
And rumor has it that we are still alive."

This spring God plants birds in heaven again,
and the wild plants bloom at once and disperse their scents,
but now, you all refuse to go back to being dust and mud.
You spirits, roam your old beloved towns with your invisible ankles,
you glare at our live sleeping bodies.

Will we be able to resist you all?
Will we be able to return you safely to death?
Divine Korea, where death and life commit incest.

우리가 당신들을 다시 낳을 수 있을까.
자자손손 거듭 낳을 수 있을까.

보이지 않는 발목들의 낮은 헤매임을
한반도 막막한 보편으로 흐르게 할 수 있을까.

Will we be able to give birth to you again?
Will we be able to give birth to your heirs generation after generation?

Will we be able to let the shallow roaming of your invisible ankles
flow across the vast reaches of Korea?

여성에 관하여

여자들은 저마다의 몸 속에 하나씩의 무덤을 갖고 있다.
죽음과 탄생이 땀 흘리는 곳,
어디로인지 떠나기 위하여 모든 인간들이 몸부림치는
영원히 눈먼 항구.
알타미라 동굴처럼 거대한 사원의 폐허처럼
굳어진 죽은 바다처럼 여자들은 누워 있다.
새들의 고향은 거기.
모래바람 부는 여자들의 내부엔
새들이 최초의 알을 까고 나온 탄생의 껍질과
죽음의 잔해가 탄피처럼 가득 쌓여 있다.
모든 것들이 태어나고 또 죽기 위해선
그 폐허의 사원과 굳어진 죽은 바다를 거쳐야만 한다.

Regarding Women

Women, every one of them has a grave inside her body.
A place where birth and death sweat,
a port forever blind,
where all humans struggle to get somewhere.
Like the Altamira cave, like the ruin of a great Buddhist temple
women lie down, a rigid dead sea.
That is the home of birds.
Sand blows inside the women.
Broken shells from the hatching of the birds' first eggs,
and the remains of death pile up like burnt blood.
The temple of ruins and the dead sea must be crossed
in order for everything to be born and die again.

오늘 저녁이 먹기 싫고

오늘 저녁이 먹기 싫고 내일 아침이 살기 싫으니
이대로 쓰러져 잠들리라,
쥐도새도모르게 잠들어 버리리라.
그러나 자고 싶어도 죽고 싶어도
누울 곳 없는 정신은 툭하면 집을 나서서
이 거리 저 골목을 기웃거리고,
살코기처럼 흥건하게 쏟아지는 불빛들.
오오 그대들 오늘도 살아계신가,
정처 없이 살아계신가.
밤나무 이파리 실뱀처럼 뒤엉켜
밤꽃들 불을 켜는 네온의 집 창가에서
나는 고아처럼 바라본다.
일촉즉발의 사랑 속에서 따스하게 숨쉬는 염통들,
구름처럼 부풀어오른 애인들의 배를 베고
여자들 남자들 하염없이 평화롭게 붕붕거리지만
흐흥 뭐해서 뭐해, 별들은 매연에 취해 찔끔거리고
구슬픈 밤 공기가 이별의 닐리리를 불러대는 밤거리.
올 늦가을엔 새빨간 루즈를 칠하고
내년엔 실한 아들 하나 낳을까
아니면 내일부터 단식을 시작할까
그러나 돌아와 방문을 열면
응답처럼 보복처럼, 나의 기둥서방
죽음이 나보다 먼저 누워
두 눈을 멀뚱거리고 있다.

Don't Want to Eat Today's Dinner

Don't want to eat today's dinner
and don't want to make it to tomorrow,
so I'll collapse as I am and fall asleep.
Mice and birds — I'll sleep without their knowing.
Consciousness that wishes to sleep, that wishes to die
has no place to rest, is liable to leave the house,
to pry around the streets and alleys.
Rays of light pour down like wet flesh.
Oh! Are you all still alive today?
Alive without a purpose?
I look out the window like an orphan
from a house of neon that lights up the chestnut flowers,
the leaves tangled like thread-snakes.
Hearts breathe snugly inside a shaky love.
Women and men vacantly buzz about in peace,
resting their heads on their lovers' bellies
that have inflated like clouds.
Ha! But what's the point? Stars drunk with smoke dribble tears,
and the street of sorrowful night air wails a farewell tune.
Shall I put on red lipstick this fall?
Shall I give birth to a robust son next year?
Or shall I start dieting tomorrow?
But when I return and open the door to my room,
my pimp-death lies down before I can,
its eyes blank
like a reply, like a revenge.

밤부엉이

밤부엉이 한 마리가 창가에서
나를 꼬나보기 시작했어.
나는 허둥거리며 내 몸의
모든 기관들을 닫아 버렸지만
부엉이의 눈빛이 오토머신처럼
내 몸 구석구석을 헤집어 열고
노란 방사선을 쏘아 부었어.
나는 사지를 늘어뜨린 채
천천히, 차갑게 용해되어 갔어.

이윽고 잠, 닫혀진 회색 강철 바다,
속으로 한 사내의 그림자가 숨어들어
내 꿈의 뒷전을 어지러이 배회하고
환각처럼 흔들리는 창가에서, 누구시죠?
내게 희미한 두통과 고통을 흘려 붓는, 누구시죠?
내 死産의 침상에 낮게 가라앉아,
누구시죠? 누구 누구 누구?...

밤부엉이가 밤새 내 지붕을 파먹었어.
아침엔 날이 흐렸고
벌어진 큰골 속으로 빗물이 뚝뚝 흘러들었어.
이미 죽은 내 몸뚱이 위에
누군가 줄기차게 오줌을 깔기고,
휘파람을 불며 유유히 떠나갔어.

Night Owl

The glance of a night owl
by the window began to dissect me.
I hurried to close down
all the organs of my body,
but the owl's glare,
like an automated machine,
dug open every nook of my body
and poured in its yellow rays.

With my limbs collapsed and scattered,
slowly, coldly I began to melt.

After a while — sleep, a locked gray steel ocean.
A man's shadow seeps inwardly,
loiters around the backstage of my dream,
and by the delirious shaking window. Who is it?
Who pours this faint ache and pain into me? Who is it?
Who sits beneath the bed of my stillborn?
Who, who, who?…

All night long the night owl fed upon my roof.
The morning was cloudy,
raindrops fell into the wide-open skull.
Someone pissed
on top of my already dead body
and then left whistling.

주인 없는 잠이 오고

주인 없는 잠이 오고
잠 없는 밤이 다시 헤매고,
애들아 이게 詩냐 막걸리냐,
겨울에 마신 술이
봄에 취하고
흘러간다 흘러가서.

나를 붙잡지 마라,
나는 네 에미가 아니다,
네 새끼도 아니다.

오냐 나 혼자 간다 가마,
늙은 몸이 詩투성이 피투성이로.
환히 불 밝혀진 고층 건물
층층이 밝은 물이 찰랑거리고
아직은 아직은이라고 말하며
희망은 뱃가죽이 땅가죽이 되도록 기어나가고
어느 날 나는 나의 무덤에 닿을 것이다.
棺 속에서 행복한 구더기들을 키우며
비로소 말갛게 깨어나
홀로 노래부르기 시작할 것이다.

Sleep Arrives Without a Dreamer

Sleep arrives without a dreamer,
and the sleepless night roams again.
You young people, is this poetry or rice wine?
The wine I drink in winter
takes effect in spring.
I float away, float.

Don't hold me back.
I'm not your mother
nor your child.

Yes, I'll go alone
in my aged body full of blood and poems.
A brightly lit high-rise —
every floor fills with radiant water.
Hope cries, "Not yet, not yet,"
and crawls out until the skin of its stomach
becomes the skin of the ground.
Some day I'll reach my grave.
I'll raise happy maggots inside a coffin
until I awake clear-headed
and begin singing to myself.

淑 에게

자본주이신 하나님은
오늘 밤에도 우리에게
저금리 신용 대부를 해 주신다.
실체 없는 꿈의 실체 있는
이자를 받기 위하여.
참 가도가도 끝없는 천국이여,
아버님 나라의 어여쁘심이여.

희망은 연한 나무잎들처럼 나부끼고
어디서 그 많은 세월의 열매들이
또 무르익었다 떨어지는데
타박타박 얼마나 더 걸어야 하는냐,
무슨 꿈에 다리 절며 그래도 가야 하느냐.

자, 내가 가진 슬픔 다 모아
한 사발의 죽을 끓였으니
함께 들자꾸나.

죽음을 향해
한 발 더,
기운차게 내딛기 위해.

For Suk

Again, tonight,
the capitalist God
offers us credit
in order to earn substantial interest
from our insubstantial dream.
Ah, endless heaven no matter how far you go,
the beauty of Father's nation.

Hope flutters like tender leaves.
From somewhere the countless fruits of time
ripen and drop again.
How far must I trudge, trudge?
Why must I limp and keep going in such a dream?

I collected my sum of sadness
and cooked up a bowl of porridge with it.
Come, have some with me.

So we can take
one more energetic step
towards death.

無 題 1

1.

나는 그들을 살아 넘겼다.
그러므로 나는 이미 내가 아니다.
이제 죽어도, 죽어서도
더 나아갈 곳은 없고

나는 이제 노래하라!
입도 혓바닥도 없이,

처음으로 마음이 찢어지고
마지막으로 항문이 찢어질 때까지
나는 이제 영원히 춤추라!
무릎도 발바닥도 없이,

노예선의 북소리 울리고
까마귀들의 습격이 시작될 때까지.

2.

구르기로 작정하면 한없이 굴러지지만,
그러나 육체는 흘러가도
마음은 흘러가지 못하며,

어머님.
저 바다 끝 너머
내 망막의 수평선에 누워 계신
종이 같은, 뿌리 없는 어머님,
가여운 내 …

내 너를 무릎 위에 얹고
가리라 가리라
앉은뱅이 시늉으로
내 너를 무덤까지 데려가리라
무덤 속에 최초로 씨 뿌리리라

Untitled 1

1.

I outlived them,
therefore I am no longer I.
If I die now, after I'm dead,
there is nowhere else for me to go out.

Now I'll sing
without mouth and tongue!

Now I'll dance forever
without knees and feet
until the heart rips for the first time,
until the anus rips for the last time!

Until the slave boat's drumming,
until the attacks by crows begin.

2.

If I decide to roll, I can roll endlessly,
and the body can drift away,
but the heart can't.

Mother!
Beyond the end of the sea,
like paper, Mother without roots
lies down on my horizon of endlessness.
My poor ...

My you, I'll sit you on my knees
and go, go,
acting like a cripple.
My you — I'll take you to the grave,
I'll scatter seeds in the grave for the first time.

(어디에도 계시옵지 않은
그대, 독기로 타오르시며
그대, 한 세상을 꺾어 버리시며
그대, 그대 그늘로 일세를 뒤덮으시며,
그러나 원하신다면,
당신이 원하는 그 깊이로
고이 추락하리라.)

3.

머나먼 소혹성 위에서
그녀가 까마득하게 외쳐댄다.
우리가 그녀의 외침을 듣지 못하는 것은,
우리가 듣고 싶어하지 않는 귀를 가진 까닭이다.
그러나 내 무의식의 코는 분명하게 찾아낸다.
이 파멸의 냄새,
보이잖게 살이 타는 푸른 냄새를.

책이 썩고
애인이 썩고
한 나라가 썩고

아랫목에서 어머니가 썩고 계시다.

4.

보이네
한밤중에
그대의 흰 죽음.

모든 事物이 까무러치고
모든 事物의 表象이 까무러치고

보이네
한밤중에
떠가는 그대의 흰 죽음.

(Nowhere to be seen, you
burn up with venom, you
break this world, you
with your shadow cover up a generation.
However, if you wish,
I'll plunge peacefully into the depths
that you desire.)

3.

From the top of a faraway asteroid
she shouts faintly.
We can't hear her
because we have ears that don't want to listen.
However, the nose of my unconscious can find it,
the smell of destruction,
the green smell of flesh burning invisibly.

A book rots,
a lover rots,
a nation rots.

On the heated floor, Mother rots.

4.

In the middle of the night,
your white death
can be seen.

All things swoon.
The emblems of all things swoon.

In the middle of the night,
your white death floating away
can be seen.

5.

　　　—그러나 언어는 여전히 하나의 울타리일 뿐이며,
　　'인간은 결국 자기 자신만을 체험할 뿐이다.'

기다려라, 이제 보다 아픈 가을이 오고
비로소 나는 그치지 않는 잠을 자기 시작하리라.
두문불출 내 마음의 세월 위에
그대들의 물음이 떨어져 내리고
떨어져 내려도
답하지 않으리라,
어느 날 문득 내 창가에 불이 꺼질 때까지.

5.

— But language is merely a barrier as always
"Ultimately one can only experience oneself"

Wait, a more painful autumn will arrive
only then I'll begin the unending sleep.
Even though their questions fall down and down
on top of the season of my confined heart,
I won't answer
until one day, suddenly the light by my window goes out.

겨울에 바다에 갔었다

겨울에 바다에 갔었다.
갈매기들이 끼룩거리며 흰 똥을 갈기고
죽어 삼일간을 떠돌던 한 여자의 시체가
해양 경비대 경비정에 걸렸다.
여자의 자궁은 바다를 향해 열려 있었다.
(오염된 바다)
열려진 자궁으로부터 병약하고 창백한 아이들이
바다의 햇빛이 눈이 부셔 비틀거리며 쏟아져 나왔다.
그들은 파도의 포말을 타고
오대주 육대양으로 흩어져 갔다.
죽은 여자는 흐물흐물한 빈 껍데기로 남아
비닐처럼 떠돌고 있었다.
세계 각처로 뿔뿔이 흩어져 간 아이들은
남아연방의 피터마릿츠버그나 오덴달루스트에서
질긴 거미집을 치고, 비율빈의 정글에서
땅 속에다 알을 까놓고 독일의 베를린이나
파리의 오르샹가나 오스망가에서
야밤을 틈타 매독을 퍼뜨리고 사생아를 낳으면서,
간혹 너무도 길고 지루한 밤에는 혁명을 일으킬 것이다.
언제나 불발의 혁명을.
겨울에 바다에 갔었다.
(오염된 바다)

Went to the Sea in Winter

Went to the sea in winter.
Seagulls stretched their necks and shat white.
The corpse of a woman floated for three days,
then was caught by a patrol boat.
The woman's vagina was opened to the sea
(the polluted sea).
Pale and sickly children poured out from her open vagina,
staggering from the sea's bright sun.
Papery skin, the remains of the dead woman,
floating like plastic.
The children rode the froth of the waves and scattered
among the oceans of five continents.
They wove sturdy spider houses
in South Africa's Pietermaritzburg or Odendaalsrus,
laid eggs in the ground of the jungles in the Philippines,
and in Berlin or Haussmann's boulevards of Paris
under cover of night they spread syphilis.
One long unbearable night they'll begin a revolution,
an invincible revolution.
Went to the sea in winter
(the polluted sea).

김혜순

Kim Hyesoon

Kim Hyesoon's (b. 1955) poetry first appeared in *Literature and Intellect*, the same journal in which Ch'oe's work also made its debut. The year was 1979 and Park Chung Hee's nearly two decades of authoritarian rule had come to an end with his assassination. However, this political transition soon brought on another coup and an oppressive military regime that lasted until the late 1980s.

Kim majored in Korean literature for her undergraduate and graduate degrees. She is a member of Another Culture (*Ttohana ŭi munhwa*), an organization which emerged in the 1980s and has played a critical role in feminist literary research and publication, including the development of women's studies in South Korea. Kim teaches creative writing and Korean poetry at Seoul College of Arts.

In 2001, Kim received the Sŏ-wŏl Poetry Award. Her book of poetry, *Poor Love Machine* (*Pulssanghan sarang kigye*) was awarded the Kim Su-yŏng Contemporary Poetry Award in 1997. Kim is the first woman to receive this coveted award. She believes that the recognition of her work was due to the emergence of women's poetry over the past few decades. Kim's poetry, among Korean contemporary women poets, is the most experimental. This experimentation is rooted in her attempt to resist conventional literary forms and language long defined by men in Korea, including the literary expectations of "female poets." In her work she explores women's multiple and simultaneous existence as grandmothers, mothers, daughters, and lovers. Her language, in the context of Korea's highly structured society, is defiant and revolutionary.

Kim Hyesoon has published eight collections of poetry; one of her most recent books is a collection of critical essays on women and writing.

The poems in translation are selected from *From Another Star* (*Tto tarŭn pyŏl esŏ*, 1981), *Father's Scarecrow* (*Abŏji ga seun hŏsuabi*, 1985), and *Seoul, My Upanishad* (*Naŭi Upanishad, Seoul*, 1994).

껍질의 노래

가르쳐주지 않아도
열려진 입술은 젖을 찾아낸다
그리곤 내 몸 속에서 단물을 빼내간다
금방 먹고도 또 빨아먹으려고 한다
제일 처음
내 입 안에서 침이 마른다
두 눈에서 눈물이 사라지고
혈관이 말라붙는다
흐르던 피가 사라지고
산천초목이 쓰러지고
낙동강 물이 마르고 강바닥이
외마디 비명을 지르며 터진다
전신이 흠뻑 빨려나간다
먹은 것을 토하면서도
열려진 너희들의 입술은
젖꼭지를 물고야 만다
마침내 온몸이 텅 비어
마른 뼈와 가죽이 남을 때까지
천궁이 갈라지고
은하수 길이 부서져내릴 때까지
아무런 생각도 떠오르지 않고
영혼마저 말라 죽을 때까지.

Song of Skin

The open lips find my breasts
though they weren't told where mine were,
draining sweet water from my body.
They want to suckle again right after they've eaten.
First, the saliva evaporates inside my mouth,
tears vanish from my eyes,
veins shrivel,
blood fades,
trees and plants collapse,
the Naktong River dries up,
and its floor shrieks as it explodes.
My whole body is pumped out.
Even though you vomit what you've just eaten,
your open lips still hang onto my nipples
till my body is emptied
of everything but dry bones and skin,
till the heaven's castle splits
and the Milky Way shatters,
till I can think of nothing
and my soul withers and dies.

귀뚜라미만큼 작아지기 위하여

눈이 내린 날, 귀뚜라미에 다가가기 위하여 우리는 엎드렸다.
엎드려서 손을 뻗쳤다.
그러나 우리의 빈 손만 허공에서 만날 뿐
귀뚜라미는 없었다.

없는 귀뚜라미에 다가가기 위하여 우리는 나뒹굴었다.
나뒹굴면서 고래고래 욕을 퍼부어댔다.
<꼬리 없는 년> <그 목소리 고운 년> <그년 나쁜 년>
그러나 허공만 픽 픽 떨어져 쌓일 뿐
귀뚜라미는 없었다.

귀뚜라미 소리를 안으려 우리는 눈 위를 뛰었다, 간절히.
눈이 내린 날, 귀뚜라미 소리에 다가가기 위하여
우리는 헐떡였다.
<우리 발자국은 왜 이리 클까?> 너는 말했다.

우리는 정말 귀뚜라미만큼 작아지고, 작아지고 싶었다.

To Become Tiny as a Cricket

The day it snowed, we prostrated ourselves to get close to a cricket.
Prostrate, we held out our hands.
There was no cricket,
only our empty hands meeting in the air.

We rolled around to get close to a cricket that wasn't there.
We rolled about, ranted and cursed,
"Tailless bitch" "Lovely-voiced bitch" "That bitch, terrible bitch"
There was no cricket,
only empty space falling in heaps and piling up.

Desperately, we ran over the snow to embrace the cricket's chirp.
We gasped to get close to the call of a cricket the day it snowed.
You said, "Why is our footprint so big?"

We wanted to become tiny, tiny as a cricket.

사랑에 관하여

1.

창문을 여시고 그대는
내 가슴에 손을 넣어
물을 퍼내셨읍니다.
도망하고 싶어 집을 나서면
그대는 어느 결에 슬며시 다가와
창문을 여시고
내 가슴 속 물을 길어 가셨읍니다.

퍼내고 퍼내시면 이윽고
한바탕의 깜깜함되어 나는 스러지고
그대는 창문을 여시고
텅 빈 가슴에
불씨를 던지며
따라와 따라와 말씀하셨읍니다.

2.

나는 그를 따라 붙는다. 악착같이 붙는다.
붙으면 도망간다, 그는. 겁을 집어먹고 도망간다.
도망가면서 나는 너의 아버지니까 접근 엄근이라고 말한다.
그러면 나는 얼른 너의 장모는 나, 바로 나라고 일러 준다.
간혹 그는 난 너의 손주다라고 말하면서 달아난다.
그러면 나는 또 얼른 나는 너의 손주 며느리다, 우리의 끈을 보이겠다고
으름장을 놓는다.
머리가 나빠진다. 나빠져서 발에 밟힌다, 머리가.
그는 사랑 때문에 산이 보이지 않는다고 너스레를 떤다.
그럼 나는 산 따위는 없고 깊은 구렁뿐인 이 세상을 몰라 보냐고 허풍을 떤다.

Regarding Love 1

1.

He opens the window,
puts his hand inside my heart,
and pumps out water.

When I open the door
because I feel like running away,
he manages to get near me,
opens the window,
and hauls the water from my heart.

As he pumps and pumps,
I stagger, blacking out,
he opens the window,
throws a hot coal
into my empty heart
and says, follow me follow me.

2.

I follow and stick close to him. I stick close no matter what.
Meanwhile, he runs away, filled with fear, he runs.
He runs and says, "I am your Father, keep your distance"
Then I let him know it's me, "I'm your mother-in-law"
Sometimes he says, "I'm your grandson," and runs.
Then I threaten right back, "I'm your grandson's wife; I'll prove our bond"
Mind deteriorates. Mind declines and is trampled.
He says smugly that because of love he can't see the mountain.
Then I brag that for me there's no such thing as mountains. Don't you see the
world is made up of nothing but deep holes?

3.

웃음이 그쳐지지 않는다.
웃을 때마다
런닝 셔츠에 구멍이 뚫린다.

푸른 마스크를 하고 당신이
들어온다.
빛나는 가위를 들었다.
마지막 말을 할 시간이야, 이제. 일어서.
당신은 말한다.

우리는 번갈아
서로의 내장을 드러낸다.
당신도 웃기 시작한다. 키득키득
키득
당, 시, 늬, 내, 장, 은, 파, 라, 쿤, 너, 무, 굴, 멌, 어
당, 시, 늬, 내, 장, 은, 노, 라, 쿤, 황, 다, 리, 야.

웃음이 그쳐지지 않는다.
웃을 때마다
옷이 사라지고
지붕이 사라진다.
여덟 활개가 늘어난다.
시린 햇빛이
웃음을 참지 못하는
당신과 나를
흔들기 시작한다.
사철나무 잎사귀들을 온 몸에 가득 달고
당신과 내가 흔들린다.

3.

My laughter doesn't stop.
With every laugh
a hole appears in a running shirt.

You wear a blue mask and enter.
You hold a pair of shiny scissors.
You say, Get up now, it's time for a showdown.

We take turns
exposing our guts.
You begin to laugh as well.
Hee hee hee
your, intestine, is, blue, is, too, skinny,
your, intestine, is, yellow, a, poisonous, moth.

Laughter doesn't stop.
With every laugh
clothing disappears,
a roof vanishes.
Eight arms stretch out.
Cold sunlight begins to shake
the two of us
unable to stop laughing.
We shake
full of evergreen leaves
attached to our bodies.

兜率歌

죽은 어머니가 내게 와서
신발 좀 빌어달라 그러며는요
신발을 벗었더랬죠

죽은 어머니가 내게 와서
부축해다오 발이 없어서 그러며는요
두 발을 벗었더랬죠

죽은 어머니가 내게 와서
빌어달라 빌어달라 그러며는요
가슴까지 벗었더랬죠

하늘엔 산이 뜨고 길이 뜨고요
아무도 없는 곳에
둥그런 달이 두 개 뜨고 있었죠

A Song: Tosolga

When my dead mother comes to me
and asks me to lend her my shoes,
I take off my shoes.

When my dead mother comes to me
and asks me to hold her up, for she has no feet,
I take off my feet.

When my dead mother comes to me
and asks to lend me, lend me,
I even rip out my heart.

In the sky, mountains rise, trails rise.
At a place where there is no one
two round moons ascend.

말

1. 마지막 말의 모양

모두 말을 해 봐요. 말이 사라지는 것을 봐요. 오늘 말들은 걸어서 저 숲 속으로 가네요. 말들이 낡은 나무 의자에 기대고 황금 기타를 치고 있네요.

불을 더 때고 한 모금 말을 해 봐요. 소리 칠 줄 알아요? 누군가 내 말을 지우고 있어요. 지워지고, 지워지고, 신문지 부스러기가 날아다녀요. 초, 록, 색, 별, 이, 부, 서, 지, 고, 있, 어, 요. 황금의 음표도 쏟아지고 어디선가 초록색 뱀 한 마리 나타나 쉼표만 골라서 먹어요. 숨이 차요. 수, 미, 차 ...

자, 같이 웃어요. 급히 웃으라니까요. 웃기라도 해야잖아요? 말들이 낡은 나무 의자와 함께 지워지려 해요. 스폰지 같은 말의 그림자만 남아서 무너지고 있어요.

　　스폰지를 사랑할 수 있어요?
　　스폰지에 물이나 먹여 봐요.
　　—잠시 캄캄함—
　　—캄캄함의 계속—

　　—모두 아, 하고 입 벌려!—

Words

1.   How the Last Words Looked

Everyone, please try to talk. Watch how speech disappears. Today's words walk away into the forest. They play a golden guitar, leaning against a worn-out wooden chair.

Feed the fire and try talking a bit. Know how to shout? Someone is erasing my words. Get erased, erased, newspaper bits are blowing about. Green, colored, star, crumbles. Golden notes fall out, and from somewhere a green snake appears and eats only the pauses. I'm out of breath. Out, of, breath …

Let's all laugh. I said laugh harder. We've at least got to laugh, don't we? Words are about to be erased together with the worn-out wooden chair. Sponge-like words crumble, leaving only a trace.

> Is it possible to love a sponge?
> Give the sponge some water.
> Temporary darkness —
> Continuation of the dark —

Everyone say Ahh, open your mouths!

말

2. 말의 긴장

다시 말할 수 있어요? 초, 록, 초, 록 냉장된 내 말이 지하실 윤전기 속에서 도는 것, 봐요.

마당에 입 대고 말해요. 네 잎 크로바가 사방 연속 무늬로 피어나고 말에는 시간 꽃이 피어요. 파도에 입 대고 말해요. 배들이 항구를 떠나고 갈매기떼 높이 그대 말이 뛰어오를 거예요.

　　냉동된 우리의 말에 주사 놓지 말아요. 주사 맞은
　　말들이 어디로 가는가 숨어서 보지 말아요.

　　—문득 벨 소리—
　　—대포 소리—

　　—모두 아, 하고 입 벌려—

Words

2. Anxiety of Words

Can you speak again? See how my green, green frozen words spin inside a basement cylinder press.

Talk with your mouth to the ground. Four-leaf clovers grow in successive patterns and time-flowers bloom as words. Talk with your mouth to the waves. Boats leave port and your words leap and rise as high as the gulls.

> Don't give needles to our frozen words. Don't hide and watch where the words go after they get their shots.

> Suddenly a bell sounds —
> Cannons roar —

> Everyone say Ahh, open your mouths!

물음표 하나

누군가 물음표에서 물음을
뽑아 버리로 있다.
닭털처럼 날리던 물음
바람에 몸을 맡긴 물음
발가벗기던 물음
온몸에 물감을 칠하던 물음
얼굴을 가린 물음
통곡하던 물음.

물음의 눈물. 눈물의 홍수. 물음의 무릎. 무릎을 당겨, 물음. 돌아누
워, 물음. 좋아, 물음. 개같이 짖어 봐, 물음. 물음, 입 벌려. 물음의
침. 침의 홍수. 물음, 무릎을 조심하라니까. 물음을 물어뜯는 물음.
잠자지 마, 물음. 노래해, 물음. 바람처럼 흩날려, 물음. 쉼표, 이리
들어와. 물음을 막아 서. 나가지 못하게 하란 말야, 쉼표. 물음, 물
음, 제자리. 노래하는 물음. 마침표를 버린 물음. 물음만 남아서 외
로운 물음. 꼬리로 만들어진 물음. 비 맞고 꼬리를 세우던 물음. 흩
날리며 입술을 깨물던 그 불쌍한 물음.

꼬리를 잃은 마침표 하나
숨죽여 울고 있다.
이제 누군가 다가가
마침표 하나에
쓰러진 물음을 쑤셔박으려 하고 있다.

A Question Mark

Someone is taking out
a question from a question mark.
Question that flew like a chicken feather,
question that gave its body to the wind,
question that stripped naked,
question that painted the entire body,
question with a hidden face,
question that cried.

Question's tears. Tears' flood. Question's knee. Pull up the knee,
question. Turn over, question. Good, question. Bark like a dog, question.
Question, open your mouth. Question's saliva. Saliva's flood. Question,
careful with the knee. Question that bites off a question. Don't sleep,
question. Sing, question. Flap around like the wind, question. Comma,
enter here. Block the question. Don't let it out, comma. Question,
question, back in place. Singing question. Question that left a period.
Question that is lonely from one remaining question. Question made up
of a tail. Question with a tail up after the rain. Oh poor question that bit
its lip while being blown about.

A period that lost a tail
cries silently.
Now someone draws near a period
and tries to shove in
a fallen question.

不眠

이것의 이름은 베개. 이것은 이불. 이것은 어둠. 어둠에 어떻게 문패를 달아 놓지? 이것은 벽. 벽은 모두 여섯 개. 하나, 둘, 셋, 넷, 다섯, 여섯, 여섯이라는것. 이것에 문패를 어떻게 달지? 내 옆에 주무시는 이 분은 어머니. 어머니는 아버지의 아내. 저 분은 아버지. 아버지는 어머니의 남편. 그러니까 아버지는 아버지의 아내의 남편. 아버지의 아내의 남편은 아버지. 화살표에 주렁주렁 문패를 매달은 나의 평면도, 봤어? 우스워. 우스움에 무슨 수로 문패를 달지? 이것은 베개, 이것은 어둠, 이것은 어머니. 잠이 안 와. 내일이면 이름 따윈 흔적도 없이 사라질 텐데. 큰일났어. 게다가 이름이란 서로 바뀌기도 쉽거든. 불면증이래나봐. 불명증? 거기다 어떻게 못을 꽝꽝 박고 문패를 달아 놓지? 잠이 안 와. 문패에 문패를 달 수도 없는 걸.

Categories of Insomnia

"Its name is Pillow." "This is a blanket." "This is darkness." "How do you hang a nameplate onto darkness?" "This is a wall." "Six walls all together." "One, two, three, four, five, six, these six. How do you hang a nameplate on it?" "The person sleeping next to me is Mother." "Mother is Father's wife." "That person is Father." "Father is Mother's husband." "Therefore Father is Father's wife's husband." "Father's wife's husband is Father." "Did you see? My flat figure, hanging drapes of nameplates on an arrow?" "It's funny." "How do you intend to hang a nameplate onto a laugh?" "This is a pillow, this is darkness, this is Mother. Can't sleep. By tomorrow names and such will vanish without a trace. We're in trouble. Besides, names get swapped so easily." "They say it's insomnia." "Insomnia? How could you pound a nail in and hang a nameplate on it?" "Can't sleep." "Can't hang a nameplate on a nameplate."

전염병자들아

—숨차게

푸르게, 시리게, 촉, 수, 만, 켜들고, 달려, 가라. 달려, 가라. 전신을,
파, 먹는, 구, 더, 기, 들에겐, 전신을, 주고, 다리, 사러, 온, 사람에겐,
다리, 팔고, 신나게, 경매를 외쳐라. 토하고, 싸고, 흘리며, 모두, 모오
두, 나눠, 줘라. 네, 심지를, 꺼내 보여라. 뛰어라. 앓는, 몸아, 너를, 부
르거든, 큰, 소리로, 살아있다살아있다, 외쳐, 대라. 도착하진, 말고,
떠, 나, 기만, 하, 거, 라. 주사, 바늘들이, 빠져, 달아나고, 희디흰, 침
대, 가, 다, 부서지도록, 피똥이, 튀고, 토, 사물과, 악취가, 하늘, 높이,
날리도록, 달리기만, 하거라. 생명이, 나갔다가들어오고, 출발했다가
도착하며, 생, 명, 을, 부렸다가다시, 지고, 또, 다, 시, 달려, 나가는 앓
는, 몸아! 저기, 저기, 쳐다봐라. 유화, 물감으로, 그려진, 행복이, 액
자, 속에, 담겨, 있고, 이제, 막, 기쁨의, 사. 카. 린.이. 강. 물. 처. 럼.
네. 피. 속으로, 들어가고, 있구나. 누군가, 살아있냐. 묻거든, 머리를,
깨부수고, 촉, 수, 를, 보여, 줘, 라.

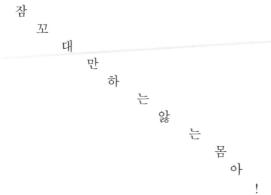

To Patients with Contagious Diseases

— breathlessly

Run, holding, only, your, lit, ten, ta, cle, blue, and, cold. Go, run.
Give, your, bodies, to, mag, gots, that, feed, on, bodies, sell, frenzied,
your, legs, to, people, who, come, to, buy, legs, and, shout your bids.
Vomit, excrete, dribble, give, away, everything, every thing. Pull out
and show, your, wick. Run. Sick, Body, when, someone, calls, you,
shout back, I'm alivealive. Don't, arrive, just, de, part. Run, so, that,
the, needles, can, slip out, white, beds, can, crumble, bloody shit, can,
splatter, and, dead things, and, stench, can, fly, high up, in, the, sky.
Life, leavesthenreturns, departsthenarrives, and, the, sick, body, burns,
up, then, takes, on, life, and, runs, out, again! Look, over there, there.
Happiness, painted, in oil, is, inside, a frame, and, now, sa. ccha. rine.
Of happiness, flows, like. a. ri. ver. Into, my, blood. If someone, asks, Is
anyone alive? Break, your, head, open, and, show, your, ten, ta, cle.
Sick
       bodies
             that
                  keep
                        talking
                              in
                                    their
                                          sleep
                                              !

딸을 낳던 날의 기억

―판소리 사설조로

거울을 열고 들어가니
거울 안에 어머니가 앉아 계시고
거울을 열고 다시 들어가니
그 거울 안에 외할머니 앉으셨고
외할머니 앉은 거울을 밀고 문턱을 넘으니
거울 안에 외증조할머니 웃고 계시고
외증조할머니 웃으시던 입술 안으로 고개를 들이미니
그 거울 안에 나보다 젊으신 외고조할머니
돌아앉으셨고
그 거울을 열고 들어가니
또 들어가니
또다시 들어가니
점점점 어두워지는 거울 속에
모든 윗대조 어머니들 앉으셨는데
그 모든 어머니들이 나를 향해
엄마엄마 부르며 혹은 중얼거리며
입을 오물거려 젖을 달라고 외치며 달겨드는데
젖은 안 나오고 누군가 자꾸 창자에
바람을 넣고
내 배는 풍선보다
더 커져서 바다 위로
이리 둥실 저리 둥실 불려다니고
거울 속은 넓고넓어
지푸라기 하나 안 잡히고
번개가 가끔 내 몸 속을 지나가고
바닷속에 자맥질해 들어갈 때마다
바다 밑 땅 위에선 모든 어머니들의
신발이 한가로이 녹고 있는데
청천벽력.
정전. 암흑천지.
순간 모든 거울들 내 앞으로 한꺼번에 쏟아지며
깨어지며 한 어머니를 토해내니
흰옷 입은 사람 여럿이 장갑 긴 손으로
거울 조각들을 치우며 피 묻고 눈감은
모든 내 어머니들의 어머니
조그만 어머니를 들어올리며
말하길 손가락이 열 개 달린 공주요!

Memories of Giving Birth to a Daughter

— in p'ansori

I open a mirror and enter,
mother is inside a mirror, sitting.
I open a mirror and enter again,
grandmother is inside a mirror, sitting.
I push aside this grandmother mirror and step over a doorsill,
great grandmother is inside a mirror, laughing.
I place my head inside great grandmother's laughing lips,
great-great grandmother, younger than me
turns around inside a mirror, sitting.
I open this mirror and enter,
enter, and
enter again.
All the ancestral mothers are sitting inside a darkening mirror,
and these mothers mutter and call in my direction,
"Mother, Mother."
Their mouths pucker, crying for milk,
but my breasts have no milk, and someone
keeps pumping wind into
my intestines.
My stomach grows bigger than a balloon,
blows here and there above the sea.
It is so wide, wide inside the mirror
that I can't even catch one blade of straw,
and sometimes lightning passes through my body.
Every time I dive into the sea
a row of mothers' shoes dissolve
on the sea's bottom.
A bolt of lightning!
Power's off! A blackout!
Suddenly, all the mirrors shatter in front of me,
and one mother is vomited out.
People in white, wearing gloves
collect the bits of mirror and hold up a small mother
smeared in blood with eyes still shut —
mother of all my mothers —
and say, "It's a ten-fingered princess!"

사랑에 관하여 2

1.

문: 눈 속에 있지?
답: 그래, 그래서 내 영혼이 매일 내 눈조리개만 보고 사는구나.
문: 영혼은 가슴속에 있을지도 몰라.
답: 그럼, 내 영혼은 내 심장만 들여다보고 사는걸.
문: 지가 무슨 공자님 맹자님이라고 사사건건 반론이야? 영혼은 어쩜 페니스 끝에 달려 있을 거야.
답: 그럼 그렇구 말구, 난 내 영혼을 자식놈을 위해 쏴 버렸다구. 난 혼도 없는 놈이야.
문: (꿈꾸듯) 영혼이란 건 어쩜 몸 속에 들어 있는 물 속에 녹아 있는 지도 몰라. 난 네가 태아처럼 웅크리고 울때 네 영혼이 눈물과 함께 조금 흘러나오는 걸 보았지.
답: 그래, 물로 되어 있을 거야. 어제 내가 내 영혼을 식탁 위에 흘려 놓았더니 그때께서 행주로 쓱싹 닦아버리던걸.
문: 어떤 이는 죽으면 영혼이 새가 되어 날아간다고 그러던데?
답: 영혼이 알 낳는 짐승이란 말은 처음 들어보는데?
문: 지금 생각해낸 건데 영혼은 몸 전체에 스며 있는 걸거야, 우린 애벌레와 같아. 죽으면 나비가 되어 날아가는 거야, 이렇게 훠얼훨! 넌 흰나비, 난 호랑나비.
답: 쳇, 하나님께서 나 같은 버터플라이 컬렉션 취미가 있는 줄 몰랐 는걸, 난 죽어서 거미가 될 거야, 특히 호랑나비 시식 취미가 있는.

2.

식은 밥에 미역국을 붓고
숟가락으로 뒤적이며, 쩝쩝 씹으며
네 영혼을 잡아두려, 찾아헤맸다
헤매다 간혹 국물 속에서 길을 잃고

Regarding Love 2

1.

Q: It's inside an eye, isn't it?
A: That's right. That's why my soul lives looking only at my irises.
Q: The soul may also be inside a heart.
A: Of course, my soul lives only to gaze upon my heart.
Q: Who do you think you are — Confucius, Mencius? You think you can dispute every point? The soul may be attached to the end of a penis.
A: Of course. You're absolutely right. I shot my own soul for the sake of my child. I have no soul.
Q: (As if dreaming …) The soul may have dissolved into my bodily fluids. When you curl up like a fetus and cry, I see a bit of your soul flowing out with the tears.
A: Yes, it must have turned to water. Yesterday when I spilled my soul on a dining room table, you wiped it off at once with a dishcloth.
Q: Some say that when a person dies, the soul becomes a bird and flies away.
A: I've never heard before that the soul is an egg-laying mammal.
Q: This is something I've just thought of. The soul must have permeated my entire being. We are like caterpillars. After we die, we become butterflies and fly away. We'll flutter away like this! You, a white butterfly, and I, a tiger butterfly.
A: Oh, I never knew God had such an interest in collecting butterflies like me. After I die, I'm going to become a spider. I'm particularly interested in tasting tiger butterflies.

2.

I pour seaweed soup over cold rice,
stir it with a spoon and chew with my mouth open,
and search everywhere to catch your soul.
Sometimes as I search I lose my way inside the soup

머리를 처박았다
영혼은 숟가락에 잡힐 듯
그러나 무거운 밥 속을 교묘히
공중 높이 가볍게, 아니
위장 아래 무겁게

3.

애벌레한마리와애벌레한마리가애벌레사랑을하는데애벌레가나비가
되어도애벌레처럼사랑할까애벌레를벗어놓고나는날아오른다신나게
애벌레를알아볼까나비가애벌레는껍질일까애벌레를벗어놓고너도날
아오르는군애벌레는어머니일까아들일까애벌레두마리와나비두마리
는어떻게서로사랑을해결할까

and shove in my head.
The soul nearly gets caught in the spoon,
but shrewdly works inside the heavy rice,
floats light on the air, no,
heavily beneath the stomach.

3.

caterpillarandcaterpillararemakingcaterpillarlovebutifcaterpillarbecom
esbutterflywillitlovelikecaterpillarIshedcaterpillarandflyhighupmadly
willbutterflyrecognizecaterpillariscaterpillarskinevenyouaresheddingc
aterpillarandflyingoverhereiscaterpillarmotherorsonhowwilltwocaterp
illarsandtwobutterfliesresolvetheirlove

너

나에게 찬물을 끼얹고는
두 주먹으로 가슴을 움켜들고 다니다가,
홍두깨로 사지를 좌악 밀어놓고는
아스팔트 위에 내동댕이도 쳐보다가,
그 위로 버스도 구르고, 탱크도 구르게
하다가, 또 싫증나면
밀가루 같은 것을 솔솔 뿌려
얼굴도 토닥거려주다가,
시퍼런 칼을 들고 나타나서는
머릿속을 쫑쫑 누비고 다니다가도
끓는 물 속에 풀썩 팽개쳐버리는,
하얗게 세어버린 내 머리카락을
물 속에 흔들어 건진 다음
양념에 무쳐 맛있게도 냠냠 칼국수를
말아먹는,
여름 한낮의

너.

You

Splash cold water over me then
walk around with my heart clenched in your two fists then
spread out my four limbs with a wooden roller then
thrash me down on asphalt then
let a bus roll over me, a tank roll over me then
if it gets tedious
sprinkle a fine powder
and fix up my face then
appear with a deep blue knife
and quilt every inch of my scalp then
discard it into boiling water then
shake and pull out from the water my hair that has turned white then
stir tasty dressing over my hair and eat it like yum yum noodles in broth
over one summer afternoon is

you.

(비)

하늘에서 투명한 개미들이 쏟아진다 (비)
머리에 개미의 발톱이 박힌다 (비)
투명한 개미들이 투명한 다리로 내 몸에 구멍을 뚫는다 (비)
마구 뚫는다 (비)
그를 떠밀면 떠밀수록 그는 나를 둘러싸고 오히려 나를 결박한다 (비)
내 심장의 화면에 투명한 글자들이 새겨진다 (비)
글자들 위에 글자들이 또 새겨진다 (비)
나는 해독하지 못한다 (비)
글자들이 이어져 어떤 파장을 그린다 (비)
새겨진다 (비)
하느님, 무슨 말씀 하시는 거에요? (비)
못 알아듣겠어요 (비)
이 전깃줄은 물이잖아요? (비)

(Rain)

Transparent ants fall from the sky (rain)
Their toenails stick to my head (rain)
Transparent ants with transparent legs dig holes in my body (rain)
Dig deeper (rain)
The more I push him away the more he pulls me to him and ties me
        up instead (rain)
Transparent words appear on the screen of my heart (rain)
Words appear again on top of the words (rain)
I cannot decipher (rain)
Words join together to create a certain wave (rain)
Appears (rain)
God, what are you saying? (rain?)
I can't understand you (rain)
Isn't this electric cord water? (rain)

이제 마악 잠이 깬 서울의 공주

한번 숨을 들이쉴 때마다
폐암에 걸린 그가
일 미터씩 침대를 뛰어오르는 것
그치지 않았는데
세면기에 물을 받을 때마다
남편의 면도날을
손목에 대보는 그녀가
아직 동맥을 자르지도 않았는데
서울대 병원 구내 소나무는 100% 숨을 못 쉰다 하더니
오늘 아침 무슨 힘으로
솔방울 하나 더 매달았는데
방통대 옆 쓰레기더미 속에서 느닷없이
똥파리 한 마리 솟아오르자
막무가내 봄이 쳐들어온다

공주는 잠을 깨어 다정하게 왕자를 바라보았다. 잠시후 두 사람은 하
늘에 걸린 탑, 카페 노란 잠수함에서 모닝 커피를 마셨다. 곤봉이 잠
을 깨었고, 잡혀가던 백성 둘도 잠을 깨었다. 세 남자는 휘둥그래진
눈으로 서로를 바라보았다. 갑자기 말들이 잠을 깨어 꼬리를 길게 늘
이며 누군가를 부르기 시작했다. 비둘기들이 꼬리 속에서 날개를 꺼
내어 두리번거리다가 마로니에 광장 저 너머로 팝콘을 찾아 걸어갔
다. 미친 라일락은 향기를 내뿜기 시작했고, 목련은 치마도 안 입고
창문부터 열었다. 왕자와 공주는 늦은 아침을 위하여 해장국집 산적
으로 들어갔다. 부뚜막의 파리가 다시 걷기 시작했고, 아궁이에서 불
길이 솟아나오며 밥이 잦기 시작했다. 프라이팬의 생선은 지글거렸
고, 요리사는 설거지 파출부에게 프라이팬을 내던졌고, 아이는 넘어
져 울기 시작했고, 그 남자는 닭털을 거지반 다 뽑았다.

막무가내 서울에 봄이 밀어닥친다
필멸의 내장 속 길로 원추리, 미나리, 봄나물이 밀려 들어오고
구절양장 굽이굽이 간판들이 내어걸린다

The Princess of Seoul Has Just Awoken

He who has lung cancer
jumps one meter above the bed
every time he breathes.
The cough's not over,
but every time a wash basin is filled
she places her husband's razor
on her wrist.
She hasn't yet cut her wrist,
but a pine tree on the grounds of Seoul University Hospital says
its breathing is not 100%.
Then with what strength did the tree attach
another pine cone to itself this morning?
Spring charges in stubbornly
as a shit-fly suddenly buzzes
up from a garbage heap next to Seoul Open University.

The princess awoke and gazed affectionately at the prince. The two
drank their morning coffee in a tower hung from the sky, a yellow
submarine café. Their morning woke up Konbongi the billy club
and two citizens under arrest who were being hauled away. These
three men stared wide-eyed at each other. Horses woke, stretched
out their tails and called to someone. Pigeons pulled out wings from
those tails and looked around, then walked over to the Marronnier
Plaza, looking for popcorn. Insane lilac started to spray its scent and
magnolia opened the window before putting on her skirt. Late in the
morning, the prince and the princess went into a spicy soup shop. A
kitchen fly walked by again, fire blazed out from the stove, and rice
began to boil. Fish in a frying pan sizzled, a cook threw the pan at a
scullery maid, a child stumbled and cried, and the cook had already
plucked almost all the chicken feathers.

In Seoul, spring charges in stubbornly.
Lilies, parsley, spring vegetables rush along
a path inside the intestine of doom.
Along a winding path street signs are posted at every turn.

막힌 나팔관 문밖에서 꼬리 달린 정자들이
문 열어요, 문 열어요 소리치고
그 남편의 아내는 다시 면도날을 집어든다
공원 아저씨가 마로니에공원의
시멘트 미로에 물을 뿌리고, 잠시 후
입구에 흰 페인트를 칠한다

몇 개의 내장을 건너가야 너를 만나게 될까
방통대 앞 까만 쓰레기 봉지 속을
수천 마리 똥파리들이 넘나들고 있다

Outside the blocked fallopian tubes, sperm shout,
"Open the door, open the door!"
and the wife of the husband grabs the razor again.
The park attendant splashes water over the Marronnier Plaza's
        cement maze,
then shortly after, he paints the entrance white.

I wonder how many intestines I must cross in order to meet you.
In front of the university, thousands of shit-flies buzz in and out
of the black garbage bag.

비 오는 날, 남산 1호 터널 들어가는 길

메추리 굽는 냄새가 공중에 떠오르지 못하고
바닥에 떨어진다
메추리 살이 빗방울과 함께
아스팔트 위에 새까맣게 탄다
앰뷸런스는 목이 쉬도록 소리치면서도
길이 막혀 빨리 죽음에 닿지도 못하는지
초록색 커튼이 안에서 열렸다 닫혔다 한다
자동차의 헤드라이트 불빛이
뭐라고 뭐라고 길에다 글씨를 쓴다
아직도 내게서 도망가지 못하는 너에게
창밖에서 배웅하는 내가 우산 밖으로 손을 내밀고 싶다
빗물로 짠 바구니를 내밀고 싶다
앞만 보고 앉은 너는 여전히
길에다 뭐라고 뭐라고 글씨만 쓴다

The Road to Mount Nam's Tunnel No. 1 on a Rainy Day

The smell of roasting quail unable to rise into the air
drops to the ground.
Quail meat burns black
with raindrops on asphalt.
An ambulance shouts until its voice fades
yet is unable to reach death in time because of traffic,
so its green curtain opens and closes from the inside.
Light beams from the headlights scribble
something, something on the road.
I see you off outside the car window.
I want to hold out my hand beyond the umbrella
to you, you who can't run away from me.
I want to hold out a basket woven with rain.
You who sit peering out the front
continue to scribble something, something on the road.

참 오래 된 호텔

참 오래 된 호텔. 밤이 되면 고양이처럼 강가에 웅크린 호텔. 그런
호텔이 있다. 가슴속엔 1992, 1993 …번호가 매겨진 방들이 있고, 내
가 투숙한 방 옆에는 사랑하는 그대도 잠들어 있다고 전해지는 그
런 호텔. 내 가슴속에 호텔이 있고, 또 호텔 속에 내가 있다. 내 가슴
속 호텔 속에 푸른 담요가 덮인 침대가 있고, 또 그 침대 속에 내가
누워 있고, 또 드러누운 내 가슴속에 그 호텔이 있다. 내 가슴속 호
텔 밖으로 푸른 강이 구겨진 양모의 주름처럼 흐르고, 관광객을 가
득 실은 배가 내 머리까지 차올랐다 내려갔다 하고. 술 마시고 머리
아픈 내가 또 그 강을 바라보기도 하고. 손잡이를 내 쪽으로 세게 당
겨야 열리는 창문 앞에 나는 서 있기도 한다. 호텔이 숨을 쉬고, 맥박
이 뛰고, 복도론 붉은 카펫 위를 소리나지 않는 청소기가 지나고, 흰
모자를 쓴 여자가 모자를 털며 허리를 펴기도 한다. 내 가슴속 호텔
의 각 방의 열쇠는 프런트에 맡겨져 있고, 나는 주머니에 한 뭉치 보
이지 않는 열쇠를 갖고 있지만, 내 마음대로 가슴속 그 호텔의 방문
을 열고 들어갈 수가 없다. 아, 밤에는 그 호텔 방들에 불이 켜지든
가? 불이 켜지면 나는 내 담요를 들치고, 내 가슴속 호텔 방문들을
열어제치고 싶다. 열망으로 내 배꼽이 환해진다. 아무리 잡아당겨도
방문이 열리지 않을 땐 힘센 사람을 부르고 싶다. 비 맞은 고양이처
럼 뛰어가기도 하는 호텔. 나를 번쩍 들어올려, 창밖으로 내던지기
도 하는 그런 호텔. 그 호텔 복도 끝 괘종시계 뒤에는 내 잠을 훔쳐
간 미친 내가 또 숨어 있다는데. 그 호텔. 불 끈 밤이 되면, 무덤에서
갓 출토된 왕관처럼 여기가 어디야 하고 어리둥절한 표정을 짓는,
자다가 일어나서 보면 내가 봐도 낯선 호텔. 내 몸 속의 모든 창문을
열면 박공 지붕 아래, 지붕을 매단 원고지에서처럼 칸칸마다 그대가
얼굴을 내미는 호텔. 아침이 되면 강물 속으로 밤고양이처럼 달아
나 강물 위로 다시 창문을 매다는 그런 호텔.

A Very Old Hotel

A very old hotel. When night arrives, the hotel crouches like a cat
by a river. There's a hotel like that. Inside my heart there are rooms
numbered 1992, 1993 … The kind of hotel that lets me know you, my
beloved, are asleep in a room next to mine. There's a hotel in my heart
and I'm inside it. Inside the hotel in my heart, there's a bed covered
with a blue blanket and I'm lying on it, and again there is the hotel
inside my heart. A blue river flowing like folds of pleated wool outside
the hotel in my heart and a boat full of tourists goes up and down in
my head. At times, I look out at the river again, head throbbing from a
hangover. And sometimes I stand in front of a window that opens only
when I pull its handle towards me. The hotel breathes, its pulse beats,
a noiseless vacuum cleaner goes over the red carpet in the hall, and a
woman wearing a white hat straightens her back as she dusts off her
hat. The room keys of the hotel in my heart are kept at the front, and
I have a bundle of invisible keys in my pocket, but I can't freely open
the rooms of the hotel inside my heart. Ah, at night, do lights come on
in the rooms of the hotel? When the lights are on, I want to kick off my
blanket and fling open the doors of the rooms of the hotel in my heart.
My bellybutton glows from burning desire. I want to call for someone
strong when the doors don't open no matter how hard I pull. The hotel
runs around like a rain-soaked cat. The kind of hotel that lifts and
throws me out the window. I heard that, crazy me, who has stolen my
own sleep, might be hiding behind a clock at the end of the hall. The
hotel. When it gets dark and the lights are off, the hotel has a confused
look of Where am I? like a crown just uncovered from a grave. The
hotel looks unfamiliar even to me when I get up in the middle of the
night. When I open all the windows inside my body, beneath the gable
roof, you stick your head out from every square as if appearing from
graph paper with a roof attached — that kind of hotel.

新派로 가는 길 3

#1   앞에서 세번째 유리창에 코를 박고
       입술을 대고 비 오는 거리를 내다본다.

#2   빨리빨리 흐르던 물살이
       화면 정지! 멈추고
#3   물길이 양쪽으로 좌악 갈라지자
#4   두 눈에 헤드라이트를 켠 메기들이
       삼렬로 양 방향 모두 정지!
#5   그러자 색색 우산 쓴 금붕어들이 건너간다
#6   아가미 밖으로 물방울 방울방울 숨 터져나오던
       저 지느러미 붉은 열대어
#7   우체국으로 미끄러져 들어간다

#8   유리창 밖으로 흐르는 눈물을 닦을 수 없는
       내가, 화면 속에서 통곡하는 그대에게
       손수건조차 건넬 수 없는 내가

#9   33번 대형 어항이 지나간 다음
#10   물길은 닫히고 물살은 빨라진다
#11   플라스틱 가로수 사이로 비 맞은 머리를 갈퀴처럼 세운
       신문팔이 치어가 지나가고
#12   한쪽 발을 질질 끄을며 중풍 든 자라 한 마리
       슬로 비디오로 왼쪽 어깨가 찌그러진다
#13   공중전화 앞에 줄 선 키싱들
       쉼없이 꼬리치면서 줄어들 줄 모른다
#14   갑자기 높은 물결이 다가와 그 줄을 산산이 흩어버린다
#15   수위는 점점 높아지지만
       손짓발짓 그대 목소리 들리지 않으므로
       난 조금도 무섭지 않다 두렵지 않다

#16   쉼없이 바뀌면서 물 깊어지는 텔레비전 화면에
       입술을 댄 내가 거리를 내다본다
       물 넘치는 거리를

The Way to Melodrama 3

#1   I press my nose and lips against the window, the third one down from the front, and watch the rain come down in the street.

#2   Fast flowing water says, "Pause it!" and stops.

#3   As the water splits in half

#4   catfish with headlights on in both eyes say,
"Everyone stop! Line up in both directions!"

#5   Then goldfish carrying rainbow umbrellas cross.

#6   Air bubbles burst out bubble by bubble from the gills of red-finned tropical fish.

#7   They slide into a post office.

#8   I can't wipe the tears that flow down outside the window.
I can't pass a handkerchief to you who lament on the screen.

#9   After a large #33 fish bowl passes by

#10   the waterway shuts down and the current picks up speed.

#11   Tiny fish, a newspaper peddler, its hair standing up like a rake, passes through an avenue of plastic trees.

#12   A fresh-water turtle drags one of its legs, for it suffered a stroke, and its left shoulder bends because of the slow video.

#13   Kissing fish line up in front of a phone booth, endlessly wagging their tails, and the line doesn't get any shorter.

#14   A strong current moves in and breaks the line to bits.

#15   The water level is rising, but I'm not scared because I don't get to hear your voice, only your silent hand-leg gestures.

#16   I press my lips against the rising water of the ever-changing television screen and look out at the street, the flooded street.

강변 포장마차

까만 쓰레기 봉지가 강변 포장마차 앞에 놓여 있다. 그 안으로 담배꽁초가 들어간다. 시들은 국화꽃이 구겨져서 들어간다. 코 푼 휴지가 들어간다. 쉰밥덩이가 들어간다. 남은 곱창이 쏟아진다. 국수 가닥이 말라비틀어져 들어간다. 지금 열차가 도착하고 있습니다. 승객 여러분은 안전선 밖으로 물러서주시기 바랍니다. 단발머리가 들어간다. 말장화가 들어간다. 백납 같은 비구니 둘이 들어간다. 취한 얼굴이 트림을 데불고 들어간다. 문이 닫히려 할 때 아이 업은 여자가 들어간다. 쓰레기 봉지 안으로 씹다 버린 껌이 들어온다. 사과 깡치가 들어온다. 까만 하늘의 별도 들어온다. 머리에 수건을 쓴 여자가 나와 봉지를 묶어놓고 들어간다. 생리대와 생선 대가리 사이에서 인광이 터졌다가 제풀에 사라진다. 뭉게뭉게 냄새가 섞이고 아이의 머리가 불끈 솟은 다음 울음소리가 터져나온다. 까만 하늘엔 까만 별이 뜨고, 파아란 하늘엔 파아란 별이 뜬다. 승객을 모두 바꾼 을지로 순환 전철은 88분 후에 정확히 강변역에서 다시 멈춘다. 까만 쓰레기 봉지가 강변 포장마차 앞에 놓여 있다. 높이 뜬 역 구내로 생리대가 올라간다. 생선 대가리가 올라간다.

A Riverside Food Stall

A black garbage bag is in front of a riverside food stall. A cigarette butt
goes into it. A withered chrysanthemum goes in scrunched up. A snot-
filled tissue goes in. Sour rice goes in. Left over tripe pours in. A dried-
out strand of noodle goes in. A train is arriving. Passengers, please
stand behind the white line. A bobbed-head gets on the train. Riding
boots get on. Two Buddhist nuns like white lead get on. A drunken
face gets on, burping. As the door is about to close, a woman carrying
a child on her back gets on. A wad of gum enters the garbage bag. An
apple pit enters. Stars of the black sky also enter. A woman wearing
a towel over her head comes out and ties up the bag and me and
then goes back inside. Between a feminine napkin and a fish head, a
fluorescent bulb bursts and dies out on its own. Rank vapors mix and a
baby's head shoots up, a cry bursts out. Black stars appear on the black
sky and blue stars appear on the blue sky. A train for Ŭljiro, carrying
new passengers, stops again exactly 88 minutes later at Riverside
Station. A black garbage bag is left in front of a riverside food stall. A
feminine napkin goes up to the elevated station. A fish head goes up.

어쩌면 좋아, 이 무거운 아버지를

애야
천년 묵은 여우는 백 사람을 잡아먹고
여자가 되고, 여자 시인인 나는
백 명의 아버지를 잡아먹고
그만 아버지가 되었구나
(망측해라, 이제 얼굴에 수염까지 돋게 생겼구나)
백 명의 아버지를 잡아먹고
그 허구의 이빨로 갈아놓은
문장의 칼을 높이 치켜들고
나 두리번거릴 때
저기서 문장의 사이로
나귀를 타고 걸어 들어오는 너의 모습
엘리엘리

너 심겨진 밭에 약을 치고 돌아온 아버지
네 팔을 잘라 나뭇단을 만드는 아버지
네 밑동을 잘라 제재소에 보내는 아버지
양손이 사나운 칼날인 아버지
큰 구두를 신어 디뎌야 할 땅도 많은 아버지
나하고 놀아요, 아버지
하면 깜짝 놀라는 아버지
나 아버지가 되기 싫어 큰 소리로 말해도
아버지의 아버지, 그 아버지를 살해했으므로 그만
아버지가 되어버린 아버지
강철 커튼 아버지 검정 잉크 아버지 기계 심장 아버지
칼날같이 갈아진 양손을 모두어야
비로소 제 가슴이 찔러지는 그런 아버지
애야, 나는 그런 망측한 아버지가 되었구나

Father Is Heavy, What Do I Do?

Child,
a hundred-year-old fox devours one hundred humans
and becomes a woman.
I, a woman poet, devour one hundred fathers
and become a father.
(How repulsive! Now I will have a five o'clock shadow)
I devour one hundred fathers,
and as I look around,
lifting high the knife of a narrative
sharpened by the teeth of fibs about the fathers.
Look at you, entering between the sentences, riding a donkey.
Eloi, Eloi!

Father returns from a field, where you are planted, after treating it
        with pesticide.
Father chops off your arm and makes a wooden platform.
Father chops off your lower trunk and sends it to a lumberyard.
Father's hands are vicious blades.
Father has acres to pace, wearing his big leather shoes.
Father is startled when I say to him, "Father, play with me!"
I shout, "I don't want to become a father!"
But Father became a father because he'd killed father, his father's
father.
Steel-curtain-father, black-ink-father, machine-heart-father.
Father has to bring his hands together sharpened like blades
in order to pierce my heart — that kind of father.
Child, I've become such a repulsive father.

자동 인화기

배추 이파리 뒤
가파른 줄기 둔덕을
배추벌레 한 마리 가고 있다
제 지나온 길 다 먹어치우며
천천히 초록길 오르고 있다
배추벌레 몸 빛깔은 먹은 길 그대로
초록이다

자동 인화기에서 사진이
한장 한장 쏟아진다
재작년 설악 대폭설 때 눈보라
그보다 더 많은 사진이
검은 통 속으로 쏟아져 들어간다
검은 눈썹이 철컥 열렸다
닫힐 때마다 내 몸 속으로 숨찬 오르막길이
쏟아져 들어온다

허리를 접었다 펼 때
저 아름다운 무용수 허리를 감싸는
사랑나비노랑나비은빛나비물결나비
저 무용수 바닥에 허리를 대고 누울 때
허리에서 비집고 나오는 나비의 껍데기들 꾸물꾸물
꾸물꾸물 나비들 날아가고 남은
밥주발 비운
검은 통에 쌓인
나비의 무거운 시체들

나 오늘의 사진들 다 먹어치우고
한바탕 꿈이었어 잠자리에 들면
저 멀리 구천 갔던
노랑나비햇살나비천둥나비검은나비 조금씩 섞여서
꿈속의 꿈으로 가끔 쏟아지면서
여기야 여기야 날 품고 날아올라
나도 한 마리 나비처럼 그대 꿈속에 언뜻 비칠까

An Automatic Film Processor

Behind a cabbage leaf
a caterpillar is scaling
a steep vein-hill.
Eating its way up,
slowly ascending a green path.
The caterpillar is green
like the path it has eaten.

Pictures pour out
of an automatic film processor.
The pictures pour into a dark container,
pile higher than last year's snow from Mount Sŏrak's big storm.
A dark eyebrow clicks open.
Every time it closes steep breathless paths
gush into my body.

When a beautiful dancer bends and straightens her waist
lovebutterflyyellowbutterflysilverybutterflywavybutterfly
embrace her waist.
When the dancer lies down with her waist touching the floor
butterfly shells squirm out from her waist — wiggle wiggle,
wiggle wiggle — the heavy remains
left by the butterflies that flew away
amass in a dark container that has
emptied its rice bowl.

I eat up today's pictures
and have a doozy of a dream, so I get into bed.
Yellowbutterflysunlightbutterflythunderbutterflyblackbutterfly
that goes far away to the world of the dead
gets mixed up and occasionally
pours down as a dream inside a dream
and says, "Here, here, embrace me and fly up here!"
I wonder if I'll also show up in your dream like a butterfly.

배추벌레 한 마리
제 길 다 먹어치우고
아무도 없는 저 하늘
배추흰나비의 길
혼자 놓아 가려고
저렇듯 안간힘 다해 초록길
먹어치우고 있다

A caterpillar
devours its own path
and paves the way of a cabbagewhitebutterfly.
It uses all its might to eat up
the green path
to go alone up to the sky
where there is no one.

블라인드 쳐진 방 4

나는 자리를 뜹니다…… 그건 네 길이지 내 길은 아니야…… 나는 의
자에서 일어납니다…… 그건 네 길이지 내 길은 아니야…… 하루 종
일 한 폭의 그림 사이로 한마디 말이 떠다닙니다 싱싱한 창에 불같이
뜨거운 뺨을 문지르고 싶습니다 싸늘한 바다였습니다 바닷속에는 더
싸늘한 우물이 깊었습니다 그 우물 곁에 낮은 집들이 잠들어 깊은 물
밖, 밤하늘로 잠꼬대를 송출중이었습니다 싸늘한 나무들이 파도에
몸을 떨었습니다 얼음같이 찬 우물에 몸을 던지고 싶었습니다 인적
없는 골목길, 그 골목길에 어두운 피가 돌돌돌 흘렀습니다…… 그건
네 길이지 내 길은 아니야…… 나는 의자에서 일어납니다…… 낮은
집들마다 높은 안테나가 매달렸습니다 안테나 끝은 바닷물을 넘었을
까? 그 보이지 않는 안테나 끝에서…… 그건 네 길이지 내 길은 아니야
…… 나는 의자에서 일어납니다…… 나는 꺼풀이요 그대는 심장입니다
아무것도 담아두려 하지 않는 주머니, 심장이 쿵쿵 뜁니다 꺼풀 속에서
끓어오르기도 합니다 어떻게 안으로 들어가지요?…… 그건 네 길이지
내 길은 아니야…… 나는 의자에서 일어납니다 블라인드 쳐진 창 아래
의자 두 개, 하루 종일 내가 번갈아 앉습니다 블라인드 쳐진 방안, 내 모
든 핏길이 그리로 뛰어들지만, 아무것도 담아놓지 않은 길 한 뭉치, 심
장으로 꽉차 있습니다

A Room with Drawn Blinds

I am getting up...... That's your path not mine...... I am getting up
from the chair...... That's your path not mine...... All day long a
phrase floats around in between the close-up's images I want to rub
my burning cheeks against a cool fresh window it was a cold sea
inside the sea there was a deep well colder than the sea   shallow
houses were asleep next to the well and transmitted their sleep-talk
outside of the deep water to the night sky cold trees trembled in the
waves I wanted to throw myself into the ice cold well an empty
alley, a stream of dark blood flowed in the alley...... That's your
path not mine...... I am getting up from the chair...... tall antennas
are attached to the roofs of the shallow houses do the ends of the
antennas reach above the sea? From the antenna ends that cannot
be seen...... That's your path not mine...... I am getting up from
the chair...... I am skin you are heart a pocket that doesn't want to
hold anything, the heart beats bam bam it boils up from inside the
skin as well how do I get inside?...... That's your path not mine...
... I am getting up from the chair the two chairs under a window in
a room with drawn blinds, all day long I take turns sitting in those
chairs inside the room with drawn blinds   all my blood-paths rush
into it, but the heart is filled up with knotted paths that hold nothing

희디흰 편지지

화창한 대낮!
느닷없이 바람 불면
뉘 부르는 소리
나 고개 획 돌려 돌아보면
문득 열리는 누옥!
방안 가득 비 오고요
아버진 아직도 구덩이를 파고 계셔요
아버지! 내 몸에서 비가 나오나봐요!
내 가슴속 흰 나무들이
한켠으로 몰려서서
바람 속에 잔가지들 털어요, 그러면서
비의 몸이 되나봐요
몸 속의 아이들이 다 물이에요
어머닌 어디 가셨나요?
밥 올려놓고 어디 가셨나요? 밥
다 타는데 어디 가셨나요?

그러나 아버지, 그 황토흙일랑 그만
파내시고 내 말 좀 들어보실래요?
내 가슴속 온갖 구멍 속의 아이들이
젖은 머리칼을 내어 말리고 그 구멍 속으로
내 편지를 가득 실은 파발마가 달려가요
내 희디흰 편지를 가득 싣고
적토마는 달려요
저기 보세요 누가 오고 있어요
큰 가방을 들었어요! 아버지
시집의 문을 닫고 마당으로 나가봐요! 우리
젖은 글씨를 햇살나무에 매달아요

A Sheet of Very White Stationery

A sunny afternoon!
I hear someone's call
when the wind blows unexpectedly,
so I turn my head,
suddenly, a shabby house opens up!
Rain's pouring inside a room,
and Father is still digging a hole.
Father! I think rain is falling out of my body!
White trees inside my heart crowd into a corner and
shake small branches in the wind,
and I think this is how I turn into rain's body.
All the children inside the body are water.
Where did Mother go?
Where did she go after boiling rice?
The rice is burning, where did she go?

But Father, please stop digging that yellow dirt,
and won't you listen to what I have to say?
The children inside all sorts of holes in my heart
are holding out their wet hair to dry,
and a post-horse loaded with my letters is running through the
holes,
a clay horse runs,
carrying my very white letters.
Look over there, someone is coming.
That someone is carrying a large briefcase!
Father, please close the book of poems and go out into the yard!
That someone is hanging our wet writing on a tree.

타클라마칸

해 떠오르면 머리를 감는 여자
허벅지가 없는 그 여자가
머리칼 위로 모래를 한 바가지 퍼 들이붓고는
첨벙 모래 구덩이에 머리를 담그는구나
발도 없는 여자가
모래강 위에서 머리를 절레절레 헹구고 있구나
가슴도 없는 여자가
머리칼도 없는 여자가
오, 몸도 없는 여자가 머리를 감고 있구나
우리 가지도 … 오지도 … 말고 … 너는 거기 … 나는 여기
무너진 나날의 메마른 머리칼이 부풀었다 펴졌다 이리저리 뒤척인다
해 떠오를 때부터 해질 때까지
없는 허리를 한번도 펴지 않고 그 여자가 머리를 감는구나
모래강의 물살을 뒤적여 빗고 있구나

Taklamakan

A woman washes her hair when the sun rises.
The woman has no thighs,
pours a bucket of sand over her hair
and plunges her head down into the sand.
The woman has no feet,
gently rinsing her hair in a river of sand.
The breastless woman,
the hairless woman,
oh, the bodiless woman is washing her hair.
We don't ... depart ... or arrive ... you're over there ... I'm over here.
The parched hair of daily disintegration puffs up then straightens
and swishes here and there.
From sunrise to sundown
the woman washes her hair without once straightening the back she
        doesn't have.
She fingers and combs the drift of the river of sand.

눈동자 속

누군가 내 눈꺼풀 속 한없는 바닷속으로
한 삽 두 삽 모래를 퍼
가라앉힌 다음
눈꺼풀을 닫고 가면

바닷속에는 물이 산발치에서 산봉우리로 흐르네
비늘 돋친 새들이 산 깊이로
깊이로 날으네
깊은 곳이 높아지고
높은 곳이 낮아지네

그곳에 밤이 오면 내 죽은 할머니들이
우리들 발밑에 찬찬히 등불을 밝히고 가네
구름은 두 발 아래 맴돌고
사람들은 바닥에 창을 매다네

아버지는 바람 속에 알을 낳고 어머니들은
나뭇가지 사이에서 새끼를 기르네
그곳의 사람들은 부지런히 산맥을 길러
육지를 세우고 달을 퍼올리네

내 한없는 바닷속 그 깊은 곳에는 참 이상한
거꾸로 된 세상이 늘 깊어 있네

Inside My Eyes

When someone shovels sand once, twice
into the endless sea under my eyelids,
then waits for the sand to settle,
closes my eyelids and leaves

water flows from the bottom of a mountain to its peaks inside the sea.
Birds spurred with fish scales fly
deep, deep into the mountain.
A deep place becomes high,
a high place becomes low.

When night arrives in that place, my dead grandmothers
calmly walk by our feet with lamps lit.
Clouds circle beneath a pair of feet,
and people tie windows onto the floor.

Father lays eggs in the wind and mothers
raise the young in the crooks of the branches.
The people of that place diligently raise a mountain range
to carve out a land, to scoop up a moon.

Deep inside my endless sea there is a very strange
upside-down world, always deep.

여자들

우리가 가지 않은 길에 대한
슬픔으로 견디겠다고 나는
썼던가 내가 사랑하는 …이라고
청승을 떨었던가 아니면 참혹한 여름이라고
엄살을 떨었던가 너 떠나고 나면 이 세상에 남은
네 생일날은 무슨 날이 되는 거냐고 물었던가
치마폭에 감추면 안 되겠냐고 영화 속에서처럼 그러면
안 되겠냐고

문을 쾅쾅 두드리며 그들은 올까
모든 전쟁의 문이 열리고
모든 전쟁의 문을 막아서며 없어요 없어요
고개를 젓는 여자들이 쏟아져나온다

치마폭에 감추면 안 되겠냐고 … 치마폭에 한 남자를 감춘 여자가 총
을 맞고 쓰러진다. 남자는 지금 막 숨이 끊어진 여자의 피를 벌컥벌
컥 마신다. 소파의 솜을 다 뜯어내고 한 여자가 거기에 그를 숨길 방
을 만든다. 피아노 속을 다 뜯어내고 한 여자가 그 속에 그의 침대를
숨긴다. 그 피아노는 건반을 두드려도 소리가 나지 않는다. 항아리에
결사적으로 걸터앉은 여자가 소리친다. 없어요 없어요 난 안 감췄어
요. 헛간에까지 쫓긴 여자가 지푸라기 속에 감춘 남자 위에 드러눕는
다. 없어요 없어요 난 안 감췄어요. 그들이 지푸라기 위에 불을 싸지
른다.

이 다음에 나 죽은 다음에
내 딸은 나를 어떻게 떠올릴까

이마를 다 뜯어내고
아무도 몰래 다락방을 만든 엄마
밤이 무거워 잠이 안 와
자다 일어나 안경을 쓰고
없어요 없어요 난 안 감췄어요
잠꼬대하는 그런 엄마

Women

Did I write that I would endure
in sorrow the path we didn't take?
Or did I put on a morbid act and say, "My beloved …"
or did I make a fuss, "It's a wretched summer"
Or did I ask, "After you depart, what happens to your birthdays yet
        to come?
What if I hid them under my skirt like in the movies?"

Will they arrive banging on the door?
All the doors of war open.
Women pour out and block the doors, shaking their heads,
"No one's here, no one's here."

What if I hid you under my skirt?… A woman who hides a man under
her skirt gets shot and falls. The man gulps down blood from the
woman who has just stopped breathing. One woman tears out all the
stuffing from a sofa and, inside it, makes a room to hide him. Another
woman tears out the insides of a piano and hides his bed inside it. The
piano makes no sound even when the keys are struck. A woman shouts
desperately sitting on the edge of a storage jar, "No one's here, no one's
here, I didn't hide anyone." A woman chased to a barn lies on top of a
man hidden under the straw. "No one's here, no one's here, I didn't hide
anyone." They set fire to the hay.

After, after I die,
how will I be remembered by my daughter?

Mommy who tore out her forehead
and secretly made an attic inside her head,
Mommy who can't fall asleep, for night is heavy.
So she gets up, puts on her glasses, and talks in her sleep,
"No one's here, no one's here, I didn't hide anyone."

비녀 꽂을 머리칼도 몇 가닥 남지 않은 할머니
지팡이에 온몸을 의지한 채
저녁마다 언덕에 올라 동구
밖 내려다보시며
민대머리 절레절레
없어요 없어요 난 안 감췄어요

무화과나무 한 그루 그 큰 손바닥으로
꽃도 안 피우고 맺은 열매를 가리고
비 맞고 서서
고개를 절레절레 흔들고 있다

Grandmother who has just enough hair left to hold up a hairpin.
Her whole weight against the cane,
she climbs up a hill every night,
looks down over the village gate,
and shakes her bald head,
"No one's here, no one's here, I didn't hide anyone."

The stump of a fig tree with that wide palm of its hand
hides a fruit formed without a flower.
It stands in the rain
and shakes its head.

이연주

Yi Yŏn-ju

Yi Yŏn-ju made her literary debut in a journal called *World of Writers* (*Chakga segye*) in 1991. The same year, Yi's first book of poetry, *A Night Market Where There Are Prostitutes* (*Maeŭmnyŏga ittnŭn pamŭi sijang*), was published by *Sekyesa*, a well-known literary press in South Korea. Yi's second collection of poems was published in 1993, one year after her suicide.

Yi Yŏn-ju is not as widely known as Cho'e Sŭng-ja and Kim Hyesoon; however, her work has been critically acknowledged by scholars and poets, including by the renowned feminist critic Kim Chŏng-nan. According to Kim, Yi's poetry has a seminal place in the feminist poetry of the 1980s. Her poetry depicts women who live on the fringes of South Korean society, marginalized by the rapid industrialization of the 1970s and 80s, which, in part, was made possible by the exploitation of young women from poor rural areas.

Not much is known about Yi. According to her brother, Yi Yong-ju, the night Yi committed suicide she had asked him to reveal nothing about her life except for her date and place of birth. Yi was born in 1953, in Kunsan in the Northern Chŏlla province. She worked in Seoul and various parts of South Korea, including Ŭijŏngbu, a U.S. military camp town north of Seoul where women and children live trapped under devastating conditions of military prostitution, environmental pollution, and poverty. She also worked for three years in Saudi Arabia. Yi received an undergraduate degree in Korean literature. She excelled in various arts and was widely known outside of literary circles by painters, filmmakers, singers, and dancers. Yi painted a great deal and was working on a collaborative video art project before she ended her life.

The poems in translation were selected from Yi's *A Night Market Where There are Prostitutes* (*Maeŭmnyŏga ittnŭn pamŭi sijang*, 1991) and *Juda, a Lamb of Redemption* (*Sokchoeyang, yuda*, 1993).

가족사진

바람난 에미가 도망치고 애비가 땅을 치고 울고

애비가 섰다판에서 날을 새고
그애비의 아이가
애비를 찾아 섰다판 방문을 두드리고

본드 마신 누이가 찢어진 속옷을 뒤집어 입고
지하상가 쓰레기장 옆에서
면도날로 팔목을 긋고

세 살 난 막내가 절룩, 절룩 자라가고
에미 애비와 누이의 일들을 거침없이 이해하고

오늘,
밤마다 도시가 하나씩 함몰되고, 나는
등불에서
등심지를 싹둑, 싹둑 잘라내고

A Family Photo

Mother's been fooling around and runs away,
father wails,
beats the ground with his fists.

Father stays up all night playing cards.
Father's child
looks for father,
knocks on the door
of the gambling room.

Sister drinks Bond glue,
wears her torn undergarments inside out,
and next to the garbage dump of a basement store
cuts her wrists with a razor.

The three-year-old baby of the family limps, limps, grows up
and quickly grasps the doings
of his mother, father, and sister.

Every night cities cave in one by one.
And today,
in front of an oil lamp,
I
snip snip off
the wick.

매음녀 1

팔을 저어 허공을 후벼판다.
온몸으로 벽을 쳐댄다.
퉁, 퉁—
반응하는 모질은 소리
사방 벽 철근 뒤에 숨어
날짐승이 낄낄거리며 웃는다.
그녀의 허벅지 밑으로 벌건 눈물이 고인다.
한번의 잠자리 끝에
이렇게 살 바엔, 너는 왜 사느냐고 물었던
사내도 있었다.
이렇게 살 바엔—
왜 살아야 하는지 그녀도 모른다.
쥐새끼들이 천장을 갉아댄다.
바퀴벌레와 옴벌레들이 옷가지들 속에서
자유롭게 죽어가거나 알을 깐다.
흐트러진 이부자리를 들추고 그녀는 매일 아침
자신의 시신을 내다버린다, 무서울 것이 없어져버린 세상.
철근 뒤에 숨어사는 날짐승이
그 시신을 먹는다.
정신병자가 되어 감금되는 일이 구원이라면
시궁창을 저벅거리는 다 떨어진 누더기의 삶은 ...
아으, 모질은 바람.

Prostitute 1

She waves her arms in the air, digging out the empty space.
Thrashes the wall with her body.
Bam, bam —
sounds a vicious reply.
A winged animal hides behind the wall's steel rods
and giggles.
Red tears collect between her inner thighs.
Once, at the end of an encounter,
there was a man who even asked,
"Why bother going on if you are going to live like this?"
If you are going to live like this —
she didn't know why she had to live.
Rats bite into the ceiling.
In between garments
roaches and maggots freely lay eggs or die.
She lifts up her disheveled bed sheets each morning
and throws out her dead body,
a world where there is nothing left to fear.
The winged animal that lives behind the steel rods
feeds on her dead body.
If salvation is becoming a mental patient and getting locked up
then the existence of worn-out rags trampling on cesspools is …
Ah, vicious wind.

매음녀 4

함박눈 내린다.
소요산 기슭 하얀 벽돌 집으로
그녀는 관공서 지프에 실려서 간다.

달아오른 한 대의 석유 난로를 지나
진찰대 옆에서 익숙하게 아랫도리를 벗는다.
양다리가 벌려지고
고름 섞인 누런 체액이 면봉에 둘둘 감겨
유리관 속에 담아진다.
꽝꽝 얼어붙은 창 바깥에서
흠뻑 눈을 뒤집어쓴 나무 잔가지들이 키들키들
그녀를 웃는다.

반쯤 부서진 문짝을 박살내고 아버지가 집을 나가던 날
그날도 함박눈 내렸다.

검진실, 이층 계단을 오르며
그녀의 마르고 주린 손가락들은 호주머니 속에서
부지런히 무엇인가를 찾아 꼬물거린다.
한때는 검은 머리칼 찰지던 그녀,
몇 번의 마른기침 뒤 뱉어내는
된가래에 추억들이 엉겨 붙는다.
지독한 삶의 냄새로부터
쉬고 싶다.

원하는 방향으로 삶이 흘러가는 사람들은
어떤 사람들일까 ...
함박눈 내린다.

Prostitute 4

Fat snowflakes are falling.
She is taken in a government jeep
to a white brick house
at the foot of Mount Soyo.

She walks past a propane gas heater,
and next to an examination bed
mechanically takes off her clothes
from the waist down.
Both of her legs open,
yellowish discharge mixed with pus
is rolled up in gauze
and placed inside a glass coffin.
Outside the hard frozen window
small tree branches blanketed in snow
cackle, cackle at her.

Fat snowflakes also fell
the day father left home shattering the half-broken door.

As she walks up the stairway
to the second floor clinic
her dry, starved fingers
search diligently for something
inside her pocket
then wriggle around the found object.
Once she had long shiny dark hair.
Memories clot around the phlegm
she spits after several dry coughs.
She wants to rest from the
stench of her vile existence.

People whose lives drift in the right direction,
who are these people?
Fat snowflakes are falling.

매음녀 5

거미집 밀창 아래 쓰레기 하치장
쓰레기 하치장 바로 옆에 키 작은 풀 언덕
언덕에 철조망, 철조망 그 위로
불 밝은 도큐 호텔

거미집에 그녀
밤이면 무덤을 나와
희미한 가등 옆에
문드러진 어깨뼈 드러내 서서

표백된 도시
불빛 내려다본다
부릅뜬 황달기의
그녀, 눈

거미집 밀창 아래 쓰레기 하치장
그 하치장 담벼락 가등 옆에
누군가의 심장, 누군가의
버려져 썩어가는 양동, 쉬었다 가세요, 네?

Prostitute 5

Beneath a paper window of the spider house
a garbage dump,
next to the garbage dump
a small grassy hill,
a metal fence on the hill,
beyond the metal fence
the brightly lit Tokyu Hotel.

The woman of the spider house
comes out of her grave at night,
stands next to a faint street light,
bares her decomposed shoulder bone,

looks down at the lights,
of a bleached city
with her
glaring jaundiced
eyes.

Beneath a paper window of the spider house
a garbage dump,
next to the light of the dump wall
somebody's heart,
somebody's discarded rotting bucket,
won't you stay for a bit, yes?

매음녀 6

어머니, 날 낳으시고 젖이 없어 울으셨다.
어머니 숨 거두시며
마음 착한 남자, 등짝 맞대 살으라 이르셨다.
나는 부둣가에서
선술집 문짝에 내걸린 초라한 등불 곁에서
매발톱 손톱을 키워 도회지로 흘러왔다.
눈 붙이면 꿈속에서 어머니
이 버러지 같은 년아,
아침까지 흑흑 느껴 우신다.
내 심장 차가운 핏톨, 썩은 물 흐르는 소리.
나는 살 속 깊은 데서 손톱을 꺼내
무덤을 더 깊이 판다.
하나의 몫을 치르기 위해 삶이 있다면
맨몸으로 던지는 돌 앞에 서서 사는
이 몫의 삶은 …
희미한 전등불 꺼질 듯 끄물거린다.

Prostitute 6

Mother cried after giving birth to me because she had no milk.
Mother told me with her last breath,
"Find a kind man and live happily ever after."
At a pier next to a dented lamp hung from a tavern door
I grew my thorny toenails, fingernails
and drifted to a city.
When I close my eyes
Mother weeps in my dream until morning, "You wormy bitch."
My heart, a cold bloody speck,
the sound of putrid running water.
I take out the fingernails from deep inside my flesh
and dig the grave deeper.
If life exists to pay off a single life
then this life
lived naked in front of the rocks thrown at you is …
The dim light flickers as if it's about to go out.

매음녀 7

이른 새벽이었네. 죽은 애기를 끌어안고 에미는 종종걸음으로 어둑
한 비탈길 내려왔네. 청소차가 방금 지나간 듯 마른 바람 한 점 횡하
니 거리를 쓸고 있었네. 건널목을 건넌 에미는 외투자락 잡아당겨 가
슴팍 핏덩어리 감추며 … 지하도 계단 앞에서 주변을 훔쳐 둘러보더
니 허둥 허둥 또 걸었네. 지친 에미곁을 느릿느릿 승용차 한 대가 지
나가고 행인들 자꾸만 눈에 밟혔네. 벌써 날이 밝았어, 벌써 날이 밝
았어, 한숨 섞어 중얼거리던 에미는 신문지에 둘둘 말아 싼 애비 모
르는 죽은 것을 쓰레기통에 쿡 처박았네. 아아, 나일론 살에 붙어 타
는 냄새.

Prostitute 7

It is daybreak. Mother clasps her dead baby and quickly walks down a dark, winding road. As if a street sweeper had just gone by, a dry wind swirls its way over the street. After crossing the train tracks, Mother pulls her jacket over her chest to hide the bloody thing … In front of a basement stairway, she peers around stealthily, then continues on her way, hurrying, hurrying. A car drives by slowly, slowly next to Mother, weary, trampling past the eyes of pedestrians. It's already daybreak, already daybreak. Mother sighs, mumbles something, then shoves her dead baby into a garbage bin, rolled up in newspaper — it has never seen its father. Ahh, the burnt smell of nylon on flesh.

좌판에 누워

나, 간 절은 자반 고등어다
홍제동 시장터에서도 도매값 팔백원이다
비늘은 죄다 떨어져 나갔다
살은 질기다.

칠백원, 어때요?
아줌마 너무하시네, 칠백오십원!

창시 빠져나간 뱃가죽 좌판에 늘어붙어
식탁으로 가는
길, 기다리는

해가 또 진다.

Lying on a Mat at the Market

I, a dried salted sardine
at Hongjedong Market,
wholesale price of 800 *won*.
All the scales have fallen off,
the flesh is tough.

"700 *won*, what do you say?"
"Lady, you're impossible, 750!"

The belly skin slipped off first
and stuck to the mat.
A road to a dinner table.
The waiting sun fades.

겨울 석양

서역, 그 뒤에도
사람이 살고 있습니까?

다시 시작해 보자.
더러운
추억의 힘이여.

Dusk in Winter

Life's end, does anyone
really live beyond it?

Let's start again.
Power of
filthy
memories.

집단무의식에 관한 한 보고서

광포한 바람이 아귀아귀 불어대는 것이었다 빗날, 폭우로 쏟아지는 것이었다. 무딘 물방울의 세포들은 전염병을 몰고 오는 바람에 쏠려 공중분해되는 격전지에서 갈쿠리 같은 병균들 와글와글 떨어지는 것이었다. 곱태낀 옛 샘터 바닥의 돌맹이들, 치욕스런 산자는 거대 자본가에게, 내 척추에 물이 마르고 있어요.

그리하여 한 밤을 자고 나면 한 사람이 망자의 인명 기록부에 이름 석 자를 남겨놓고 그리하여 한 가족이 파라티온을 마시고 한 마을이 서로의 목을 졸라 살상 행위의 범법자가 되어가는 것이었다. 자살자에 대한 간략한 보도에 살아 있는 개별자들은 수전증을 앓는 늙은이처럼 벌벌 손이 떨려 드디어 가면 공장이 문을 열고 땅을 기는 하류 짐승들의 촉수가 잘려져나간 가면들이 봉고차에 실려 슈퍼마켓으로 바쁘게 배달되는 것이었다.

날마다 사이렌이 불어대는 것이었다. 자살 집회의 봉쇄를 위한 수만 명의 전경이 광장에 배치되고 사복 경찰들은 골목골목에서 무전기를 들고 대문간 안을 기웃거리는 것이었다. 저녁식사를 마친 아버지가 포르노를 보는 동안 술취한 아들이 화장실 변기통에 똥물을 토해대는 동안 가면 속에서 은밀하게 술렁거리는 그들은 건초더미 마르고 까슬까슬한 저녁나절의 꿈을 꾸는 것이었다 집단 파리떼의 주검.

A Report on the Unconsciousness of the Masses

Frenzy, a famished wind blows. A day of rain arrives in a torrential downpour. The cellular matter of dulled raindrops, swept up by the wind that hauls in contagious diseases, dissipates in the air over a battle zone. Hoards of hooked germs fall. Phlegm-covered pebbles on the floor of an old spring. A person living with shame says to the great capitalist, "My spinal fluid is drying up."

Then after a night of unbroken sleep, someone leaves a name — three syllables — in an archive of the dead, and as a result an entire family drinks the pesticide Parathion, and the people of a certain village wring each other's necks, transformed into murderous criminals. Those who are abuzz with news of the suicide watch their hands shake as severely as someone suffering from Parkinson's. And a mask factory opens its doors, and the masks of inferior land-crawling animals with severed tentacles are loaded into a van and promptly delivered to a supermarket.

Every day sirens wail. A view of the populace, a blockade for a suicide assembly is arranged in a public square, and plain-clothes police on every alley, carrying wireless receivers, peep into houses. A father who has finished his dinner watches porno, while his drunken son vomits into a toilet bowl, those who are secretly agitated inside the mask dream a prickly, dry-as-hay, late-afternoon dream. The dead remains of the collective mass of houseflies.

지리한 대화

그 탱자나무 울타리, 어머니 생각나세요?
이젠 네 아들이 거기서 놀 게다, 네가 뜻을 바꾸거라.
희뜩하니 문지방까지 내려온 하늘 ... 나는 중얼거리며
돈과 안락한 생활이 모든 인간을 만족시킬 수는 없어요, 어머니가
절 포기하세요.
나는 너를 낳고 온몸에 두드러기로 고생했다.
알아요, 그러셨어요.
바느질감을 내려놓으시며 어머니, 긴 한숨이 차고 슬프다.
나는 시계를 본다,
왜 이렇게 어수선한지 모르겠군요, 날 좀
내버려둬요.
가족을 버리겠다는 거냐?
가족이 나를 필요로 하진 않아요, 벌써 오래된 일이잖아요.
그건 네가 환상을 꿈꾸어 왔기 때문이야,
이제라도 뜻을 바꾸면 행복해질 게다.
행복? 그래요, 행복 ...
하늘은 매양 왜 저 모양인지, 나는 집을 나선다.
한곳으로 몰리던 바람이 저만치 날 밀어다 놓고 골목길 접어
사라진다
멍든 곳을 훤히 드러낸 나무들 몸통은
어떤 힘으로 겨울을 버티는 걸까.
어머니, 이 손톱 끝을 좀 보세요, 아직도 가시에 찔린 자죽이
시퍼런걸요.

148

A Tiresome Dialogue

"Mother, do you remember the orange tree fence?"
"Now your son will get to play around that fence, you need to change your ways."
Something bright, it was the sky that came down to the sill. I mumble …
"Money and the easy life won't satisfy everyone. Mother, you should give up on me."
"I was covered in hives after I gave birth to you."
"I know, you suffered."
Mother puts down her sewing, her sigh cold and sad.
I look at the clock. "I don't know why things are so complicated, please leave me alone."
"Are you saying you want to abandon your family?"
"The family doesn't need me. It's the same old story."
"That's because you've been deluding yourself. If you change your ways, you can be happy."
Happy? All right, happy …
I leave the house. Why is the sky always like that? The wind comes up and pushes me aside then blows into the alley and disappears.
The trees that expose their bruises — with what strength do they endure the winter?
"Mother, see my fingernails. The scars from the thorns are still blue."

라라라, 알 수 없어요

왜 헬리콥터는 창을 흔드는가
너는 왜 블라인드를 내려놓고
오하이오 즉흥 따위의 반극을 읽고 있는가
그리고 너는 왜 기를 세워놓고
아, 그리고 왜 깃발 속으로

깃발 속에서 나부끼네
빌딩과 루핑집들이
뚝뚝 끊어지는 팬 필터의 소리를 내며
불연소성 시간 속에서

이상한 입방형의 방정식을 풀고 있는
찬우며 영자 미경이며 충렬아, 너

볼모로 잡혀 어리광떠는 삶 아닌가
게걸스럽게 검은 우유나 빨아대는
예술이라는 코카인은 270여 개나 되는
잡뼈들을 괄시해 왔었지 그런데, 왜
헬리콥터는 오늘도 창에 와서 ...

La La La, There is No Way of Knowing

Why does the helicopter shake the window?
Why are you pulling down the blinds
and reading such an anti-play as the *Ohio Impromptu*?
And why have you raised the flag?
Ah, and why go inside the flag?

Buildings and houses on top
flutter inside the flag,
making the clicking sound of a fan
inside an inflammable hour.

Ch'an-u, Yŏng-ja, Mi-kyŏng, Ch'ung-nyŏl
are all solving a strange math equation.

Existence, are you playing cute because you've been taken hostage?
Cocaine, so called art, voraciously sucks up black milk
and has been contemptuous to 270 tiny bones, but why
has the helicopter come again today, hovering by the window, and?…

집행자는 편지를 읽을 시간이 없다

친애하는 선생,
이 도시엔 경계망이 대단하오.
하루 세 번 교대되는 경비 초소의 무장 군인들
시간은 촘촘한 그물망처럼 규격이 단단하오.
소통은 벌써 끊겼소이다, 거리마다 화농한 살덩어리
불그스름한 피고름이 질펀하오.
주민들은 몰지각 발작 증세를 보이기 시작했소.
몇 그램의 몰핀과
몇 박스의 신경안정제를 부탁하는 바이오.
싸움이 무슨 쓸모가 있겠소.
산자들에 의해 죽은자의 시신은 매일 밤 소각된다오.
공문서의 철이 두터워가는 건 수모일 뿐이지요.
살균제의 씩씩함이란
여기선 끝장난 일 아니겠소.
바람이 심하게 부는구려.
병균을 실어 나르는 데 이보다 더 좋은 매체는 없지요.
전염 속도를 지연시킬 방책을 또 찾아봐야겠지만
문제는
선생,
이 편지 역시 서랍 속에 던져지기 십상이라는걸 ...

An Executioner Doesn't Have Time to Read a Letter

Dear Sir,
The city is heavily guarded.
Armed soldiers rotate
posts three times a day.
Their hours, their mandate is as rigid as a dragnet.
Communication has already been cut off.
Every street is infested with decaying flesh,
crimson bloody pus.
Civilians are beginning to show signs of hysteria.
Several grams of morphine and
several boxes of tranquilizers have been requested.
What would be the point of fighting?
Those who are dead because of those alive,
their bodies incinerated each night.
The official document files are growing thicker, a mere insult.
Isn't this the end of the power of disinfectants?
The wind is blowing hard.
There is no better medium than this for delivering germs.
I need to find a method to delay the spread of germs once more, but
Sir,
the problem is
you are most likely to bury this letter inside a desk drawer …

가나마이신 에게

주저앉은 코뼈를 몇번이나 갈아 끼웠는지
일본산 실리콘을 미제 파라핀을
오똑한 콧날에 기여한 수입된 자긍심은
얼마나 즐거웠던지

가끔 철사로 찌르는 듯한 아픔과
눈팅이까지 부어오르는 부작용쯤이야

선진적 시민의식을 밀어주는
가나마이신이여!

좌, 우를 갈라놓은 두 개의 콧구멍 속 어디선가
영악한 이물질이
제 전통의 뼈를 조금씩 갉아 먹어가는 것을 모른 채
총을 뽑아드는 경찰의 강력 처방으로
가짜의 위안과
가짜의 안도감

염증이 너무 심하면 죽을 수도 있다잖나.

For Kanamycin

Don't know how many times the flat nose-bone has been replaced.
Silicon made in Japan, paraffin made in the USA
accentuating the bridge of the nose.

Oh, the joy of imported self-pride
except for the occasional pain that feels like a wire's jab
and the side effect of swelling all the way to the eyes.

Kanamycin,
you promote advanced consciousness among the citizens!

Somewhere inside the two nostrils
that divide left and right
you ignore the ferocious matter
that eats away the entire bone bit by bit.
With the powerful remedy of a policeman
pulling out a gun,
gain false solace,
false relief.

You can die if the infection is serious.

끌과 망치가 필요한 때

한 남자가 웅크리고 앉아 있었다 그 어깨가 크고 작은 진동음을 내며 흔들렸다 한 남자가 울고 있었다. 두 남자가 어둑한 골목 쪽에 서 있었다. 자살 게임처럼 그들은 서로를 큰 주먹으로 쳤다 자리를 옮겨가며 서로의 가슴과 옆구리를 질렀다. 진열장 안에서 마네킹이 비틀거렸다 어린 여자들은 제 또래 남자애의 외투 속으로 파고들어 가며 쿵쿵거리는 발자국 소리 무서워 밤엔 왜 더욱 크게 들리는 걸까 ... 여자애의 입 속으로 그 또래 남자들은 혀를 밀어넣어 그들은 딱딱한 불감증을 나누었다. 벽을 뚫고 나가기 위해선 끌과 망치가 필요하지 벽은 단단하고 철근과 콘크리트로 굳어져 있으니까. 길 가던 나는 생각했다 그런데 어디를 가야 우리들의 뚱뚱해진 몸을 덤으로 얹어주며 끌과 망치를 구할 수 있는 걸까, 하늘은 주린 듯 펄럭이고 은박지로 부서지는 별들 ...

When in Need of a Chisel and Hammer

One man sat, stooped over. His shoulders quivered in silence.
Another man cried. Two men stood in a dark alley. In a suicide game,
they struck each other with massive fists. Stabbing each other in
the side and chest, they switched positions. Mannequins inside the
display box staggered. And young women hid under the overcoats of
young men their age. "The thunder of footsteps is terrifying. Why is
it louder at night?" The young men pushed tongues into the mouths
of young women, and they shared a hard, disturbing sensation. You
need a chisel and a hammer to break a hole through the wall because
it is reinforced with concrete and steel. As I was walking I thought,
"But where must we go in order to turn in our lump of fattened flesh
for a chisel and a hammer?" The sky fluttered as if it were starved and
the stars crumbled into silver confetti …

독재자

내 일기책은 두 권—반항과 복종
열린 마음인 양 한 권은 사무실 책상 위에
숨통에 꾸려 감춘 다른 한 권에서는
도둑질 같은 땀이 괸다

반항과 복종이라는 두 명의
나는 어른이 되었네
이스트를 넣어 부풀린 삶 속에서
밀 덩어리를 반죽하듯 —일기책

반항적 남성은 복종이 기쁨인 여성을 지배한다
흐르는 강물과 사계절은
지하실 납골당의 뚜껑 깨진 푸른 단지

두 갈래 습관의 혓바닥이 쓰네
노동의 참신한 내 하루,
도둑질 같은 땀을 훔치며
도망치는 보상 없는 내 하루

두 명의 나를 길러 끌고가는 나는
집단심리를 제대로 쓰는 재벌 아닌가?
어느새 나는 민중이라는, 내,
독재자가 되어 있다.

The Dictator

My diary is in two parts — resistance and obedience.
One is an open heart on top of my office desk
and the other is shoved inside a throat,
a cold sweat gathers inside.

Now I'm a grown-up
with a yeast-bloated existence
as if working dough.
The diary of two beings — resistance and obedience.

A dominant male subdues a female
who finds happiness in obedience.
A flowing river and the four seasons
are a blue jar with a broken lid in a crypt.

The tongue of divided habit tastes bitter.
My new day of labor, a day of loss,
running away in a cold sweat.

I drag along the two of me I've raised.
Could I be the corporate class
proficient in manipulating group psychology?
Already I've become the populace,
the dictator of myself.

비극적 삼각관계

암탉 같은 어머니 모로 누워 계신다.
짧은 벼슬을 내려놓고
쭈글쭈글해진 배를 땅바닥에 철퍼덕
모가지를 조여대는 출산에 쓰이는 천조각

막 낳은 단조로운 흰 달걀 하나가
아직 뜨끈뜨끈한 김을 내며
아버지, 저를 죽여주세요
긴장형 조발성 치매증을 앓고 있다.

긴 장화를 신고 난자를 멸시하셨지
휘청거리는 해골을 덜렁덜렁
상스럽게 쓰던
아버지, 아버님, 오, 무자비한 …

어머니 짧은 벼슬을 푸르르 떨며
어쩌다가 씨앗이 우리를 경멸하게 되었는가.
흘러가던 구름 몇점이
똥을 찍—갈기고 간다.

A Tragic Triangle

A hen-like mother lies on her side,
sets down her modest crown.
Her creased belly flops,
a rag for strangling,
for receiving a child.

A common white egg just laid
still gives off steam,
"Father, please kill me."
It suffers from anxiety, insanity.

Father, dear father, oh merciless …
wore high rubber boots,
discriminated against an ovum,
and repulsively put on a skull
which swayed, dangled.

Mother quivers her modest crown,
"How did one sperm get to despise us so?"
A few passing clouds rain down shit
then drift away.

폐물놀이

우리는 버려진 시계나 고장난 라디오
헌 의자카바나 살대가 부러진 우산이다

못쓰는 주방용품 오래된 석유난로 팔아요
낡은 신발짝이나 몸에 안 맞는 옷가지들
짐이 되는 물건들 삽니다

우리는 구겨진 지폐와 몇개의 백동전
우리는 끊어진 전선줄이다

수신도 송신도 없다

Festival of Waste

We are discarded clocks or broken radios,
old car seat covers or umbrellas with severed frames.

We sell useless kitchenware, old gas furnaces.
We buy worn-out shoes, clothes that don't fit,
any burdensome goods.

Crinkled bills and discolored coins, we are.
Cut wire, we are.

No transmission, no reception.

인큐베이터에서의 휴일

1.

위장병이 도졌다
예감이 좋질 않아
건강해지고 싶어 벽에 걸린 사진 속의 자살자가 말한다
네 친구가 되고 싶다.

2.

창과 틀 사이 엇물린 시간
오후 2시
나는 빨랫줄에 걸린다
생선뼈와도
…
죽는 일에 자신이 생긴다는 것은 무엇일까

3.

오늘 석간신문의 머릿기사는
종신형을 받은 그를 무엇이 천대했는가
독나방이를 죽인다
왜 나는 부정하는 것만이 아름다울까
단단해져 가는
아우슈비츠의 비누쪽들

A Holiday Inside an Incubator

1.

Had a relapse of stomach and bowel disorder.
Have a bad feeling about it.
"I want to become healthy," says the one
in the photo, hung on the wall, who'd
committed suicide.
I want to be your friend.

2.

Time skewed in between the sill and the window.
It is 2 in the afternoon.
I get hooked on a clothesline
with fish bones.

What is this thing about having confidence in dying?

3.

Today's evening paper's headline:
RECEIVES LIFE SENTENCE
WHAT WENT AGAINST HIM?
I kill a poisonous moth.
Why do I find beauty only in the defiled?

Bits of Auschwitz soap
harden.

무엇이 잘못?

한 젊은 여자가 난관절제수술을 받았습니다
망원렌즈가 달린 복강경이 아랫배 깊숙한 곳을 파고들 때
퀘퀘한 지하도를 빠져나온 듯
상쾌한 느낌이었습니다
이너저분한 판국에 무슨 배짱으로 자식새끼를 …
한 젊은 여자가 생각합니다
종양의 뼈마디에 아가방 우주복을 입혀
암세포의 응어리를 키운단 말인가
한 젊은 여자가 오늘 난관절제수술을 받고
장롱 밑구멍으로 들어가 눕습니다
애기집으로 가는길 싹둑 잘라버리고 나서
그날, 밤새도록, 웬일일까요
속이 메스껍고 머리 속이 웅웅거립니다
이차원의 사고력은 일차원에서 시작되겠지요?
생각해 봅시다
삼차원의 결단과 일차원적 갈등의 거리 너무 멀어
저녁 짓는 밥냄새는 알약처럼
김을 내뿜을 겨를 없이 익어버린 것 아니겠어요?
오늘 한 젊은 여자가
자식 낳는 일이 차마 이젠 못할 짓이라고
난관절제수술을 받고 돌아왔습니다
그리고 바퀴벌레처럼
장롱 밑구멍에 누워 저렇게 조용한 것입니다.

What's Wrong?

One young woman had surgery to become childless.
When the speculum was pushed deep into her lower belly
she felt a refreshing sensation as if she'd escaped from a stuffy subway.
I'd have a lot of nerve having kids in this mess
thought the young woman.
Do I dress up a tumor-filled joint in baby clothes
so I can nurture a cancerous cell?
Today one young woman is sterilized,
and she crawls beneath a wardrobe and lies down.
What's wrong?
After cutting off the path to a baby's womb
she feels nauseous and her head throbs all night long.
Doesn't a second diagnosis stem from a first?
Let's think.
The difference between the third diagnosis and the first is so great
that don't you think the second diagnosis has ripened
like the pills that smell of boiling rice without
a moment to let out its steam?
Because she can no longer bear giving birth to a child,
today one young woman has returned home after being sterilized.
She lies down beneath a wardrobe, is as quiet
as a roach.

출산 에피소드

애 머리가 절반쯤 나오고 있습니다
분만중인 산모가
몸을 벌떡 일으키며 지나치다 싶게 갑자기
호들갑을 떱니다

머리가 둘은 아니죠? 팔은 셋은 아니죠? 눈, 코, 입,
제대로 다 있는 거죠?

아기 울음소리가 공기를 찢습니다
의사가 시간을 알립니다
속이 허해진 산모, 기어들어가는 목소리로

애가 이상하면 죽이세요.
에어콘이 붕붕붕붕 탁음을 내며 돌고 있습니다.

A Birth Episode

About half of the infant's head is out.
The woman giving birth
gets up abruptly
and gestures.

It doesn't have two heads, right?
It doesn't have three arms, right?
It has eyes, a nose, and a mouth
all in the proper places, right?

The infant's cry rips the air.
The doctor announces the time.
The woman, now emptied, speaks in a faint voice.

"Please kill the baby if it's not normal"

The air conditioner makes a humming noise *bungbungbungbung.*

얕은 무의식의 꿈

어머니, 숨겨주세요, 무서워요, 저, 구둣발 소리, 개떼를, 몰고, 오나
봐요, 어머니, 어디로, 어머니, 살려줘요, 어제도, 한 달 전에도, 이웃
집 청년이, 이층집 남자가, 사라지고, 돌아오지, 않았잖아요, 저들이,
으으, 어머니, 유리창에, 내, 얼굴이, 눈이, 무서워요, 내 손이, 웬일인
지, 조금씩, 움직여요, 아, 나는, 가만있는데, 손이, 움직여요, 문고리
를, 열잖아요, 개떼가, 아, 몰려오는, 구둣발 소리, 그들은, 겁탈할 거
예요, 그들은, 짓이길 거예요, 어디, 먼데로, 도망쳐요, 어머니, 어디
계세요, 나도 모르게, 그들과, 내가, 아, 난 싫어요, 뭐라구요, 이제는,
살아 있는게, 죄라니요, 도망칠 수, 없다니요, 그럼, 나는, 아으!

Dream of a Shallow Unconscious

Mother, please hide me, I'm afraid, that, sound of footsteps, maybe they are, herding, a pack of dogs, to here, Mother, go where? Mother, help me, just yesterday, just a month ago, a young man in the neighborhood, the man on the second floor, disappeared, they haven't, returned, they, uhh uhh, Mother, my, face, eyes, reflected in the window, are terrifying, my hand, is moving, unexpectedly, bit by bit, ahh, even though, I'm, not moving, the hand, is moving, it's unlocking, the door, the pack of dogs, ahh, a troop of footsteps, are coming, they'll, rape, they'll, crush, let's run away, somewhere, far, Mother, where did you go, without me knowing? I should, with them, ahh, I don't want to, what did you say? that it is a sin to be alive? that we can't run away? then, I'll, ahh uhh!

신생아실 노트

방치된 탄생이 관 같은 요람 위에 누워 있다. 푸줏간의 비릿한 냄새,
온갖 경험을 거쳐 늙은이의 침묵에 이르기까지 누가 저것들을 그 먼
곳까지 인도할 수 있으리. 나는 세면대 가득 물을 받아 손을 씻는다.

이곳은 불을 끄면 그대로 암흑이다. 어제 태어난 아이도 자궁 감자로
끄집어냈지 않나, 모두가 그렇다. 아니면 마취제를 전신에 걸고 절개
수술로써 태어남의 시분초를 알리는 것이다, 전쟁터에 일개 보병으로
올려지는 시간이지. 나는 어린것 하나를 들어올려 벌써 노랗게 곪아
가는 그 얼굴의 반점들을 지켜본다.

이것 봐, 총과 칼로써 네 몸을 무장하는 거야 어렵지 않지, 문제는 맨
몸으로 기도문 한 구절 없이 버티는 용기와 저항의 힘이란다. 기도문
이란 다만 죽은 자들을 위한 문장일 뿐이니까 … 나는 알코올솜으로
정성들여 손바닥을 문지른다. 제발 잊지 말아, 저 전깃불이 얼마나 큰
어둠을 감추고 있는지 …

Nursery Notes

Just born and already neglected, it lies in a coffin-like cradle. Smells fishy as a butcher's shop. Who will be able to guide the infants to a faraway place, through the many trials of life until they reach the silence of the aged? I fill up the basin and wash my hands.

When the lights are off, this place remains in darkness. Even the infant born yesterday was pulled from the uterus like a potato; it's like that. Or the entire body is anesthetized for a cesarean and the time of birth is announced, the hour when an infant is sent out onto a battlefield like a foot soldier. I pick up an infant and watch the spots on its face fill with yellow pus.

Shielding your body with guns and knives is not difficult, the problem is finding the strength to resist, naked and without a single prayer. But then prayers are only written for the dead ... I rub my hands briskly with a cotton ball soaked in alcohol. Please don't forget how thoroughly the light hides the immense darkness ...

Translator's Notes

Portrait of von Ka-kya

Ka-kya are two Korean vowels. *Yŏŭi Island* is surrounded by the Han River, which flows through the capital of South Korea. The island was once used as a military airport, but it was converted in the early 70s into a governmental and corporate sector.

Happy Diary

Assarabia Toroamitabul is a Buddhist mantra

A Song: *Tosolga*

Tosolga is a four-line song composed in the Silla period (28 C.E.). This song is recorded in one of Korea's oldest documents, *Memorabilia of Three Kingdoms* (*Samgukyusa*), written by the Buddhist Monk Ilyŏn (1206-1289). Two suns appeared side by side and remained in the sky for ten days; the song was composed to prevent any calamity to the kingdom.

Memories of Giving Birth to a Daughter

P'ansori is a Korean traditional folk narrative. It is performed by a drummer and a singer. The singer assumes the characters' various roles, using a fan as the only prop.

Prostitute 5

During the 70s in South Korea, hotels were built to attract foreign currency via Japanese tourists. In these hotels, young Korean women, mostly from poor rural areas, were exploited in government-sponsored prostitution.

La La La, There is No Way of Knowing

Ohio Impromptu is a play by Samuel Beckett written in the early 1980s. Ch'an-u, Yŏng-ja, Mi-kyŏng, Ch'ung-nyŏl are common proper names.

For Kanamycin

Kanamycin is an antibiotic.